OPPOSING VIEWPOINTS®

CRIME AND CRIMINALS

Other Books of Related Interest

OPPOSING VIEWPOINTS®

CRIME AND CRIMINALS

James D. Torr, *Book Editor*

Bruce Glassman, *Vice President*
Bonnie Szumski, *Publisher*
Helen Cothran, *Managing Editor*

OPPOSING
VIEWPOINTS®
SERIES

GREENHAVEN
PRESS®

THOMSON
————————————™
GALE

San Diego • Detroit • New York • San Francisco • Cleveland
New Haven, Conn. • Waterville, Maine • London • Munich

© 2004 by Greenhaven Press. Greenhaven Press is an imprint of Thomson Gale, a part of the Thomson Corporation.

Thomson is a trademark and Gale [and Greenhaven Press] are registered trademarks used herein under license.

For more information, contact
Greenhaven Press
27500 Drake Rd.
Farmington Hills, MI 48331-3535
Or you can visit our Internet site at http://www.gale.com

Cover credit: © Digital Stock

LIBRARY OF CONGRESS CATALOGING-IN-PUBLICATION DATA

Crime and criminals : opposing viewpoints / James D. Torr, book editor.
p. cm. — (Opposing viewpoints series)
Includes bibliographical references and index.
ISBN 0-7377-2222-3 (lib. : alk. paper) — ISBN 0-7377-2223-1 (pbk. : alk. paper)
1. Crime—United States. 2. Crime prevention—United States. 3. Criminal justice, administration of—United States. I. Torr, James D., 1974– . II. Series.
HV6789.C68133 2004
364.973—dc22   2004042416

Printed in the United States of America

> "Congress shall make no law...abridging the freedom of speech, or of the press."

First Amendment to the U.S. Constitution

The basic foundation of our democracy is the First Amendment guarantee of freedom of expression. The Opposing Viewpoints Series is dedicated to the concept of this basic freedom and the idea that it is more important to practice it than to enshrine it.

Contents

Why Consider Opposing Viewpoints?

"The only way in which a human being can make some approach to knowing the whole of a subject is by hearing what can be said about it by persons of every variety of opinion and studying all modes in which it can be looked at by every character of mind. No wise man ever acquired his wisdom in any mode but this."

John Stuart Mill

In our media-intensive culture it is not difficult to find differing opinions. Thousands of newspapers and magazines and dozens of radio and television talk shows resound with differing points of view. The difficulty lies in deciding which opinion to agree with and which "experts" seem the most credible. The more inundated we become with differing opinions and claims, the more essential it is to hone critical reading and thinking skills to evaluate these ideas. Opposing Viewpoints books address this problem directly by presenting stimulating debates that can be used to enhance and teach these skills. The varied opinions contained in each book examine many different aspects of a single issue. While examining these conveniently edited opposing views, readers can develop critical thinking skills such as the ability to compare and contrast authors' credibility, facts, argumentation styles, use of persuasive techniques, and other stylistic tools. In short, the Opposing Viewpoints Series is an ideal way to attain the higher-level thinking and reading skills so essential in a culture of diverse and contradictory opinions.

In addition to providing a tool for critical thinking, Opposing Viewpoints books challenge readers to question their own strongly held opinions and assumptions. Most people form their opinions on the basis of upbringing, peer pressure, and personal, cultural, or professional bias. By reading carefully balanced opposing views, readers must directly confront new ideas as well as the opinions of those with whom they disagree. This is not to simplistically argue that everyone who reads opposing views will—or should—change his or her opinion. Instead, the series enhances readers' understanding of their own views by encouraging confrontation with opposing ideas. Careful examination of others' views can lead to the readers' understanding of the logical inconsistencies in their own opinions, perspective on why they hold an opinion, and the consideration of the possibility that their opinion requires further evaluation.

Evaluating Other Opinions

To ensure that this type of examination occurs, Opposing Viewpoints books present all types of opinions. Prominent spokespeople on different sides of each issue as well as well-known professionals from many disciplines challenge the reader. An additional goal of the series is to provide a forum for other, less known, or even unpopular viewpoints. The opinion of an ordinary person who has had to make the decision to cut off life support from a terminally ill relative, for example, may be just as valuable and provide just as much insight as a medical ethicist's professional opinion. The editors have two additional purposes in including these less known views. One, the editors encourage readers to respect others' opinions—even when not enhanced by professional credibility. It is only by reading or listening to and objectively evaluating others' ideas that one can determine whether they are worthy of consideration. Two, the inclusion of such viewpoints encourages the important critical thinking skill of objectively evaluating an author's credentials and bias. This evaluation will illuminate an author's reasons for taking a particular stance on an issue and will aid in readers' evaluation of the author's ideas.

It is our hope that these books will give readers a deeper understanding of the issues debated and an appreciation of the complexity of even seemingly simple issues when good and honest people disagree. This awareness is particularly important in a democratic society such as ours in which people enter into public debate to determine the common good. Those with whom one disagrees should not be regarded as enemies but rather as people whose views deserve careful examination and may shed light on one's own.

Thomas Jefferson once said that "difference of opinion leads to inquiry, and inquiry to truth." Jefferson, a broadly educated man, argued that "if a nation expects to be ignorant and free . . . it expects what never was and never will be." As individuals and as a nation, it is imperative that we consider the opinions of others and examine them with skill and discernment. The Opposing Viewpoints Series is intended to help readers achieve this goal.

David L. Bender and Bruno Leone,
Founders

Greenhaven Press anthologies primarily consist of previously published material taken from a variety of sources, including periodicals, books, scholarly journals, newspapers, government documents, and position papers from private and public organizations. These original sources are often edited for length and to ensure their accessibility for a young adult audience. The anthology editors also change the original titles of these works in order to clearly present the main thesis of each viewpoint and to explicitly indicate the opinion presented in the viewpoint. These alterations are made in consideration of both the reading and comprehension levels of a young adult audience. Every effort is made to ensure that Greenhaven Press accurately reflects the original intent of the authors included in this anthology.

Introduction

"The number of very tenable explanations for the crime drop [of the 1990s], none of which inherently excludes any of the others, leads to the conclusion that . . . a variety of factors . . . have been important."

—*Alfred Blumstein and Joel Wallman,*
The Crime Drop in America

The good news on crime is that, since 1993, the United States has been experiencing a sweeping decline in crime rates. According to the Justice Department's National Crime Victimization Survey, between 1993 and 2002 the violent crime rate decreased 54 percent, from fifty to twenty-three victimizations per one thousand persons age twelve or older. Rape and sexual assault decreased by 56 percent during this period, robbery rates fell by 63 percent, and aggravated assaults (assaults associated with weapon use or serious injury) were down 64 percent between 1993 and 2002. The property crime rate declined 50 percent, from 319 to 159 crimes per one thousand households. The household burglary rate fell 52 percent; the motor vehicle theft rate fell 53 percent; and the attempted motor vehicle theft rate fell by 71 percent. "No one knows how long the crime drop . . . will extend," write Henry Ruth and Kevin R. Reitz in *The Challenge of Crime.* They add, "we do know from history that a long crime recession is possible."

The crime drop that began in 1993 is cause for optimism—and a topic of much research. If criminologists and other researchers can explain why crime fell in the 1990s, then hopefully legislators and law enforcement organizations can use that knowledge to craft policies to help keep crime rates down. However, as Ruth and Reitz note, "Guesswork about the future is greatly complicated . . . by the fact that no one fully understands the reasons for the contemporary crime drop." In general, there is no single explanation for why crime rates rise or fall, and there are many theories why crime rates began falling in the 1990s. However, amidst all the possible explanations, four factors stand out.

First, many researchers maintain that the crime drop of the 1990s was closely tied to the booming economy of the mid- to late-1990s. Unemployment rates dropped throughout this period, from almost 7 percent at the start of 1993 to 4 percent at the end of 1999. A study by Boston's Initiative for a Competitive Inner City found that median inner-city household incomes grew by 20 percent between 1990 and 2000. With increased job opportunities and higher wages, individuals may have been less likely to turn to crime to support themselves. If crime rates are closely tied to the economy, however, there is cause for concern since unemployment and poverty rates began rising in early 2000.

A second factor that is believed to greatly affect U.S. crime rates is the availability of firearms. The relationship between gun ownership and crime rates is highly controversial, and anti- and progun groups have each posited their own different theories for how guns affected the crime drop of the 1990s. Antigun groups argue that gun control measures such as the 1994 Brady Law—which mandates criminal background checks for gun purchasers—have helped lower crime rates by keeping guns out of the hands of criminals. Progun groups, on the other hand, point out that gun ownership rates rose in the 1990s, and they argue that citizens often use guns to stop criminals. In essence, antigun groups say that crime rates have fallen because fewer criminals have access to guns while progun groups maintain that crime rates have fallen because more law-abiding citizens own guns. Each side can point to various statistics to support their view, and both claims may have merit.

A third factor behind the drop in crime rates is the illegal drug trade. The crime drop that began in 1993 was preceded by a steep rise in violent crime from 1985 to 1991. Much of the violent crime of the late 1980s was associated with drug trafficking—particularly the trade in crack cocaine. Many criminologists contend that crime rates are generally higher both among drug addicts, who turn to crime to support their habits, and drug dealers, who often use violence against rival drug syndicates. The crack cocaine epidemic of the late 1980s resulted in particularly high levels of violent crime, and many researchers associate the crime drop of the 1990s with the decline of crack cocaine as the drug of choice among the urban poor.

Finally, the crime drop of the 1990s may also be due in part to tougher crime policies. Since the 1970s, the United States has increased the severity of the penalties for most types of criminal offenses, particularly drug trafficking. After a nationwide halt on capital punishment in 1972, thirty-eight states have reinstated the death penalty. Moreover, in addition to increasing the number of years a convict may serve for a particular offense, legislators have also instituted mandatory minimum sentences for many crimes, removing judges' power to adjust prison sentences based on the circumstances of the crime. The result is that the United States has the highest incarceration rate in the world, with more than 2 million Americans behind bars. Many critics argue that America's prison policies are unjust, but supporters maintain that they have played a large role in the crime drop.

These four factors—the economy, firearm ownership, the illegal drug trade, and tougher sentencing laws—are intertwined in ways that make it difficult to study them individually. For example, high rates of gun violence may be associated with high rates of drug abuse, and high rates of drug abuse may be associated with hard economic times. Longer prison terms may keep criminals off the street, but they may also result in more hardened prisoners who are prone to unemployment, drug abuse, and crime once they are released.

Crime and Criminals: Opposing Viewpoints examines the factors behind the recent drop in crime in the following chapters: What Causes Crime? Does Controlling Guns Control Crime? How Should the Criminal Justice System Be Reformed? How Can Crime Be Reduced? The authors in this anthology offer differing views on why crime rates rise and fall as well as a variety of perspectives on how the criminal justice system can best keep crime rates down in the future.

CHAPTER 1

What Causes Crime?

Chapter Preface

The debate over what causes crime is important because it is directly tied to the debate over what policies can best reduce crime. For example, if alcoholism and drug abuse tend to cause criminal behavior, then zoning laws that restrict the number of liquor stores in an area or increased policing in neighborhoods where illegal drugs are sold may help reduce crime. If unemployment and poor wages contribute to crime, then crime rates might be lowered through government efforts to stimulate the economy and relieve poverty.

A fundamental division in the debate is whether crime is really "caused" by socioeconomic factors such as poverty or unemployment. Social conservatives tend to view crime as the result of individual choice, and they reject the idea that poverty, inequality, or family dysfunction may be to blame. For those who share this view, crime is an immoral act that deserves to be punished rather than a social problem that the government should try to solve. Charles Logan, a professor of sociology at the University of Connecticut, writes that conservatives tend to argue that "felonies are wrong and controllable acts, and those who commit them will be punished" while liberals tend to argue that "felonies are the result of social and personal deficiencies (of opportunity, knowledge, skills, habits, temperament, and so on), and society has a responsibility to correct those deficiencies."

John Klofas, a professor of criminal justice at the Rochester Institute of Technology, argues that in the United States, the conservative view of crime has largely prevailed. "We are more comfortable thinking of criminality as a characteristic of individuals." Klofas believes that Americans tend to ignore the underlying socioeconomic causes of crime: "We are uncomfortable thinking our, or other's, behavior has been influenced by economic status or neighborhood. . . . We prefer to ignore the factors that produce crime in our poorest neighborhoods. We have no programs to address them."

The viewpoints in the following chapter examine several social factors that may influence crime and offer suggestions on how the criminal justice system should deal with them.

"Wherever neighborhoods are plagued by extreme poverty and unemployment, extraordinarily high levels of violent crime exist."

Poverty Causes Crime

George Winslow

George Winslow is a journalist and the author of *Capital Crimes*, a book that discusses how the global economy affects crime rates. In the following viewpoint Winslow argues that crime is more a matter of economics than morality. Although the dominant view of crime in the United States is that crime is the result of individual criminals making bad decisions, the reality is that crime is largely a product of poverty. Street crime is most rampant in poor neighborhoods, and crime rates rise and fall in proportion to how the national economy is doing. Well-paying jobs, concludes Winslow, are far more effective than police or prisons in reducing crime.

As you read, consider the following questions:
1. As of 1991, what percentage of prison inmates earned less than fifteen thousand dollars per year prior to their imprisonment, according to the author?
2. In Winslow's view, how have U.S. tax policies affected urban poverty?
3. According to the author's statistics, by what percentage did wages for black men in their twenties fall between 1973 and 1989?

George Winslow, "Capital Crimes: The Political Economy of Crime in America," *Monthly Review*, vol. 52, November 2000, p. 38. Copyright © 2000 by Monthly Review Press. Reproduced by permission.

American politicians have been declaring victory in the war against crime at least since Richard Nixon said in 1972 that "crime . . . [is] finally beginning to go back down . . . [because] we have a remarkable record on the law-and-order issues, with crime legislation . . . and narcotics bills." In other words, crime declines because the government passes laws and spends money; larger prisons, more police, fewer civil liberties, and tougher punishments are winning the war on crime.

There is no question that more stringent laws and larger expenditures are the government's strategy. Federal, state and local spending for law enforcement jumped from six billion dollars in 1968 to 120.2 billion dollars in 1996, and may top two hundred billion dollars by the 2004 presidential election. And these numbers don't include the 210 billion dollars spent by businesses and individuals on security systems, insurance, and other measures to protect themselves from crime. Supporters of all this spending point to the dramatic decline in the number of homicides (from a peak of 24,700 in 1991 to about 16,900 in 1999) and in violent crimes (from a peak of 4.1 million in 1994 to about 2.8 million in 1998) as proof that the war is being won.

Unfortunately, there is one problem with the notion that our law-and-order crusade is winning the war on crime. It isn't true. The crusade was a dismal failure for many years. Violent-crime rates jumped 89 percent between 1972 and 1991, and victimization rates showed little improvement between 1973 and 1991. Even with recent declines in crime, the one trillion dollars spent by law-enforcement agencies in the last thirty-five years only managed to reduce the 1998 homicide rates to what they were in 1967, when Nixon traveled around the country claiming that "America has become among the most lawless and violent [nations] in the history of free people."

These dismal statistics exclude many of the world's deadliest crimes. While U.S. drug use has declined, levels of addiction remain high and the global drug market continues to expand. Back in 1970, when Nixon declared war on heroin, the entire world produced about one thousand tons of opium a year. By 1973, Nixon was declaring that "we have turned the corner [in the war against drugs]," but opium production continued to increase. Today, global opium production is four times higher than it was in the early 1970s, and United Nations (U.N.) officials estimate that the global drug trade tops three hundred billion dollars. . . .

The Roots of the Problem

To avoid repeating this hugely expensive failure, it is important to ask fundamental questions about the causes of crime. In recent years, most American politicians have simply offered a few stock answers—violent Hollywood movies, permissive liberal ideas, the changing American family, and a general decline in traditional moral values. This has not only produced disastrous policies; it has also shifted the debate away from one of the key causes of crime: corporate power.

In the last half-century, corporate investment decisions have exacerbated the social problems that create crime—such as poverty and joblessness—and transformed the workings of the global economy, making it easier for criminals to launder money, pollute the environment, and expose their employees to dangerous working conditions. Some of the critical economic theories of the left, which emphasize the accumulation of capital, class relations, and imperialism, can help us examine some of the world's deadliest crimes.

The right never tires of exonerating society and blaming crime on the criminals. This is, of course, nonsense. To understand the important role that basic social and economic problems play in the creation of street crime, simply take a map of a major American city and put a small red dot wherever a homicide occurred. Soon small red lakes start forming in the city's poorest neighborhoods. For example, in 1993, the New York City Police Department reported that twelve of the city's seventy-four precincts—all twelve located in impoverished areas of Harlem, the Bronx, and Brooklyn—reported a total of 854 homicides (43.6 percent of the city's 1,960 murders) while twelve other precincts—all located in more affluent terrain—reported only thirty-seven homicides (less than 2 percent of the total). In general, wherever neighborhoods are plagued by extreme poverty and unemployment, extraordinarily high levels of violent crime exist.

Not surprisingly, U.S. prisons are also filled with convicts who have little formal education, lousy job prospects, and dismal incomes. One government survey of prisoners who entered state prisons in 1991 found that 64 percent had not graduated from high school, compared to 19.8 percent in the general population. About 45 percent did not have a full-time job when they were arrested, 33 percent were unemployed, about 70 percent earned less than fifteen thousand dollars a year (compared to 23.5 percent of all U.S. households), and only 15 percent earned more than twenty-five thousand dollars a year (compared to 59.2 percent of all American households).

Race and Inequality

Likewise, inmate populations are mostly people of color that have faced severe socioeconomic problems. Blacks, with unemployment rates twice as high as whites and poverty rates more than three times higher, comprise 30 percent of federal and 46 percent of state inmates, even though they make up only 12 percent of the U.S. population. Latinos, suffering unemployment rates nearly twice as high as whites and poverty rates nearly three times higher, make up 28 percent of federal and 17 percent of state inmates, but just 10.2 percent of the population. In short, the higher incarceration rates of blacks and Latinos are very strongly correlated with their higher unemployment and poverty rates.

The link between poverty and crime, however, needs to be handled with care. There is, for example, no evidence to support the view that young males of color and immigrants are "more criminal" than other members of the population. Most impoverished young men manage to get through life without committing serious violent crimes, and those who do enter a life of crime commit few of the worst crimes. Most corporate crimes are committed by wealthy, middle-aged white men, and young people of color have virtually no control over the global drug trade or money-laundering. The popularity of derogatory stereotypes also obscures the terrible impact that street crime has on less-affluent neighborhoods. We tend to forget that working and less-affluent Americans are disproportionately victimized by crime. This is particularly true of corporate crime—poorer neighborhoods generally have the worst environmental problems, and working Americans are far more likely to die at work than more affluent white-collar workers. In addition, about half of all U.S. homicide victims are black. People who live in households that have less than fifteen thousand dollars in annual income are three times more likely to be raped or sexually assaulted, two times more likely to be robbed, and one and a half times more likely to be a victim of an aggravated assault than those who live in wealthy households.

International Child Poverty

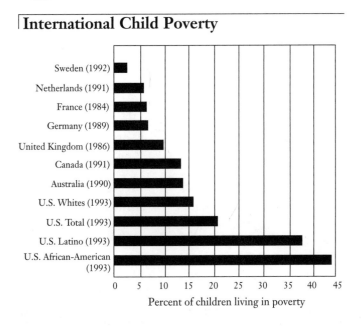

Percent of children living in poverty

Steven R. Donziger, *The Real War on Crime*. New York: HarperPerennial, 1996.

All of this goes to show that the salient difference between high-crime and low-crime neighborhoods in urban centers is economics, not morality. Communities that offer their residents economic and social opportunities have low rates of street crime. And it also tells us why hiring more police, building more prisons, and imposing tougher sentences has not worked. Spending on law enforcement has increased astronomically and the number of people behind bars now approaches two million, but there is little evidence that punishment has had much of an impact on crime rates. Crime rates rose in the 1960s, when the number of people behind bars fell, but those numbers rose in the 1970s as the prison population skyrocketed. Street crime rates then fell in the early 1980s, as the prison population soared. But, crime rates escalated dramatically between 1984 and 1992, when the prison population increased even faster and even more draconian laws were passed. Crime rates dropped in the mid-1990s, as still more people were put behind bars. While law-and-order fanatics have taken credit for this decrease, any honest observer can see there is no connection between stiffer punishment and lower crime rates.

Prisons have been ineffective because punishment doesn't address what might be crudely called the supply of criminals. Government officials can double or triple the number of people behind bars and keep them there for longer periods of time, as they have in recent years. But crime will not decrease as long as social and economic problems create millions of new street criminals to take their place.

Poverty and Crime in the Twentieth Century

The effects of economic changes on crime can be seen in the recent history of poor white immigrants in major cities like New York. In the 1910s and 1920s, for example, Irish, Italian, and Jewish neighborhoods had extremely high rates of street crime. At the time, conservative commentators blamed the problem on genetics. Yet, a mere two generations later, the grandchildren of these supposedly degenerate races are generally affluent and well-educated, with low unemployment rates. Not surprisingly, their involvement in street crime has also plunged.

The success of these groups and the failure of others can be traced to the economic changes made during the New Deal in the 1930s and the early postwar period in the 1940s, which expanded the consumer economy, boosted wages, and improved educational opportunities. But these benefits were not spread equally throughout the economy.

For starters, U.S. farm policies, which encouraged the development of a capital-intensive agribusiness, pushed millions of small farmers and farm laborers out of the U.S. South, Appalachia, and Puerto Rico into Northern cities between 1940 and 1970. These new immigrants arrived at a time when government policies and corporate investment strategies were encouraging the flow of capital out of the older industrial cities and into the lower wage, nonunion urban centers and suburbs of the South and West. Massive U.S. military spending encouraged an enormous government-sponsored shift of capital from urban centers to either the suburbs or low-wage centers abroad. Domestic military spending during the Second World War was disproportionately made in suburban or Sunbelt areas, and the vast majority of postwar military spending occurred outside of urban centers.

Meanwhile, tax policies such as the interest deduction for mortgages favored suburban homeowners over urban renters and reduced investment in decaying urban housing stocks, while other aspects of the corporate tax code encouraged corporations to build new factories overseas or in the suburbs rather than remodel and upgrade urban facilities.

Over time, these capital movements destroyed the economic basis of many American cities and pushed up crime rates, despite the country's overall prosperity. In one study, Don Wallace and Drew Humphries investigated crime rates in twenty-three cities between 1950 and 1971. They looked at the connection between different types of crime and larger economic changes, such as a region's economic prospects, labor-force changes, levels of poverty, and unemployment and analyzed how this affected different types of crime. Overall, they found that older, industrial cities had lost jobs, suffered high unemployment, faced large numbers of new migrants, and had much higher levels of murder, robbery, auto theft, and burglary. They concluded: "This result supports our hypothesis as well as earlier studies linking industrial employment, community stability and low crime rates."

Such problems were further exacerbated in the late 1960s and 1970s. Faced with growing international competition, higher oil prices, and worldwide economic stagnation, corporate America underwent a painful restructuring. Layoffs, attacks on organized labor, the movement of factories overseas to low-wage zones, reduced government regulation, probusiness tax policies, and a wave of mergers cut overhead, boosted profits, and created more globally competitive corporate behemoths. This increased the prosperity of the richest Americans, but it also caused family incomes to stagnate, poverty rates to remain high, and wages for low-skilled workers to drop.

The Crime Boom of the 1980s

The economic restructuring of the 1970s and 1980s had an enormous impact on street crime, and not just in the cities. In the 1980s, crime became an increasingly worrisome problem in both rural and suburban areas as millions of workers lost their jobs, the manufacturing sector was devastated, and real wages fell dramatically. Still, America's cities and their low-wage and often minority workers suffered the most. Overall, almost three million manufacturing jobs were lost nationwide in U.S. cities between 1979 and 1990. Moreover, pay for many low-skilled jobs in the United States fell dramatically—a particularly important development because men with few skills and little formal education are much more likely to commit street crimes than other demographic groups. Wages for low-skilled white men in their twenties fell by 14 percent between 1973 and 1989, while wages for white high-school dropouts fell by 33 percent. Similarly, wages for black high-school dropouts fell by 50 percent and those for black men in their twenties fell by 24 percent during this period.

These problems were compounded by the right's successful attacks on social programs designed to eradicate the causes of crime. Between 1981 and 1992, federal spending for subsidized housing fell by 82 percent; job training and employment programs were cut by 63 percent; and the budget for community development and social service block grants was trimmed by 40 percent. Between 1972 and 1992, welfare and food-stamp benefits for single mothers declined by an average of 27 percent nationwide. Although welfare benefits once provided enough money for a family of four to live at the poverty level, no state in the early 1990s (when crime rates hit record highs) provided grants and subsidies equal to 100 percent of the poverty level.

Reduced wages, higher unemployment rates, and lower government benefits played a crucial role in the rise of street crime and the growth of street drug markets. Likewise, improved economic conditions in many cities after 1993 begin to explain the recent reductions in street crime. It is no coincidence that street crime rates have fallen to their lowest levels in thirty-five years in a period when unemployment and poverty rates have also dropped back to the levels last seen in the more prosperous 1960s.

"The best way to restore communities and lessen poverty is to reduce crime itself, not the supposed 'root causes' of crime."

Poverty Does Not Cause Crime

Eli Lehrer

In the following viewpoint Eli Lehrer takes issue with the argument that poverty causes crime. While it is true that crime rates are generally higher in poorer neighborhoods, Lehrer maintains that many such neighborhoods are not crime-ridden because they are poor but are poor because they are crime-ridden. Citing examples from neighborhoods across the country, he argues that customers avoid shopping in high-crime areas, and entrepreneurs in turn avoid starting businesses in neighborhoods where people are afraid to walk on the street at night. In neighborhoods where a strong police presence has reduced crime, the economy has flourished. Rather than trying to boost a city's economy in order to create jobs and reduce crime, Lehrer writes, cities should crack down on crime in order to rescue neighborhoods from poverty. Lehrer is a Bradley Fellow at the Heritage Foundation where he studies crime and urban policy.

As you read, consider the following questions:
1. By what percentage did crime fall in Boston's Hyde Square in the 1990s, according to Lehrer?
2. In the author's opinion, why don't existing business owners in poor neighborhoods necessarily benefit from crime-reduction efforts?
3. What term does sociologist Elijah Anderson use to describe the culture of aggression and violence that pervades crime-ridden neighborhoods?

For most of the past 35 years, conventional wisdom has held that poverty causes crime. "Warring on poverty, inadequate housing, and unemployment is warring on crime," wrote the members of the 1967 Presidential Commission on Law Enforcement and the Administration of Criminal Justice. In college sociology courses, such thinking still dominates discourse: Steven R. Donziger's *The Real War on Crime*, an influential book published in 1996, concludes that "a program to reduce poverty levels . . . will reduce levels of crime and violence and make the country safer." In 1999, a widely publicized report from the Milton S. Eisenhower Foundation came to much the same conclusion, arguing that well-run social programs for everyone, from at-risk youth to recently released prisoners, would mitigate the effects of poverty and, thus, reduce crime.

Yet a substantial body of criminological research over the past 20 years suggests that the relationship between poverty and crime runs counter to conventional wisdom. Social scientists such as John J. DiIulio, Jr., James Q. Wilson, Wesley Skogan, Leo Schuerman, and Solomon Korbin have shown that, in fact, poverty and neighborhood degradation often result from crime—not the other way around. Skogan, a Northwestern University criminologist who has studied what happens to places where crime and disorder increase, describes a scene of utter desolation: "These areas are no longer recognizable as neighborhoods."

I spent several months traveling to low-income areas around the country to investigate whether reductions in crime led to neighborhood renewal. My firsthand experience only reaffirmed the new thinking on poverty and crime: In short, when crime drops drastically, low-income neighborhoods come back to life. Commercial strips blossom with new businesses, housing improves, streets become safe at night, mediating institutions become stronger, and disorder vanishes from public spaces. Thus warring on crime is the best way to remedy a wide variety of social ills, and America's success in reducing crime ranks with welfare reform as the greatest social policy triumph of the 1990s. . . .

To study the effects of crime reduction on civil society, I visited nine different neighborhoods in the cities of New

York, Los Angeles, Boston, Garden Grove, California, and Providence, Rhode Island. I included New York and Los Angeles because they are the country's two largest cities and have reduced crime significantly. (Between 1994 and 1999, New York reduced crime nearly 45 percent; Los Angeles about 41 percent.) I selected the other three cities because they have reduced crime more than the average for cities similar in size and character. (Providence's reductions actually fall below the national average but are larger than those in most other small-center cities in the Northeast.) . . .

I made three stops in Boston. The Four Corners, Dorchester neighborhood is synonymous with the name of Reverend Eugene Rivers, who decided to work there in the early 1980s because it was so troubled. Between 1990 and 1999, serious crime rates have dropped nearly 70 percent for the mostly African-American neighborhood of about 28,000. Boston's Hyde Square, Jamaica Plain neighborhood once qualified as a war zone, but its 12,000 residents saw crime fall about 50 percent between 1990 and 1999. Boston's Upham's Corner, a Dorchester neighborhood of 24,000 residents, has also seen crime fall over 50 percent since 1990.

I made three stops in California, two in Garden Grove and one in Los Angeles. Garden Grove's Stewart Drive neighborhood was out of control by the early 1990s. Crime rates in this ethnically mixed neighborhood dropped by half for the area's 2,100 or so residents between 1995 and 1998. In 1983, the *Los Angeles Times* called Garden Grove's Buena-Clinton neighborhood "Orange County's Worst Slum." Yet crime has fallen around 50 percent. In the late 1980s, the residents of Yucca Corridor in Los Angeles often slept on the floor to avoid gunshots from rival gangs. Today, the neighborhood of about 8,500, just steps away from the tawdry glitz of Hollywood Boulevard, has a new park, scores of new community activities, and much improved housing. Crime rates fell over 40 percent between 1994 and 1999.

In Providence, Rhode Island, serious crime in the Armory District has fallen nearly 60 percent since 1989. Investment by the Armory Revival Company, a private, profitable concern with revenues that averaged about $7 million a year in the late 1990s, has transformed the neighborhood from a collection of burned-out hulks into a vibrant area of about 4,500.

New York's Alphabet City, a Lower-East Side Manhattan neighborhood, hit bottom when Ed Koch's administration sent in SWAT-team-like anti-drug forces under the mostly ineffective Operation Pressure Point in the late 1980s. Since then, the crime-fighting efforts of Rudy Giuliani and a series of new investments have slowly transformed Alphabet City from an open-air heroin market and campground for the homeless to a gentrifying area full of nightspots and boutiques. Crime has decreased about 65 percent since 1990 for the neighborhood's 70,000 residents.

By the early 1980s, The Bronx's Hunt's Point was one of New York's most desolate neighborhoods. The infamous Fort Apache police station sat on a plot of land where rampant arson had reduced several acres to prairie. Today, the once barren area around Fort Apache contains prosperous looking single-family homes, and vacancies have nearly vanished along the Southern Boulevard commercial strip. Official crime rates fell a bit over 30 percent between 1990 and 1998 for the area's 50,000 residents. But neighborhood leaders point out that Hunt's Point experienced significant population growth in the 1990s, so safety has probably increased more than statistics indicate. After a population crash in the late 1970s, the area grew faster than any other in New York during the late 1980s, and fast growth continued in the 1990s.

Reducing Crime Pays

All of these neighborhoods consist overwhelmingly of people with low-to-moderate incomes: Poverty rates range between 20 and 55 percent, and a majority of students at local schools qualify for free or reduced-price lunches. Alphabet City, Hyde Square, and the Armory District—all well-located neighborhoods endowed with good housing stock and parks—have begun to see a sizable influx of young professionals and families, but remain mostly low-income by local standards.

For people living at the bottom of the economic ladder, commercial opportunities are quite limited. For such individuals, the improvements in the consumer economy stimulated by reductions in crime tend to make an enormous difference. When crime drops, the prospects of stores large enough to attract customers who don't live within walking distance improve. But since many neighborhood stores sell liquor and thrive when people fear leaving the few blocks they know best, such businesses see fewer positive effects. Shopping strips, however, benefit from a longer shopping day, reductions in merchants' fears, increased competition, and an influx of new types of business.

How Crime Taxes the Poor

Many economists think of crime as a tax on urban life. In this regard, it proves particularly cruel; the "crime tax" actually charges the poor a higher rate than the wealthy. The Bureau of Justice Statistics' National Crime Victimization Survey shows just how much crime hurts the poorest Americans. For the 30 million or so Americans living in households earning less than $15,000 a year, crime represents a horrific fact of daily life. Compared to the middle class, the poor fall victim to nearly six times as many rapes, more than twice as many robberies, almost double the number of aggravated assaults, and half again more acts of theft. Crime is, in short, an inversely progressive tax.

Eli Lehrer, "Crime-Fighting and Urban Renewal," *Public Interest*, Fall 2000.

Through the 1970s and 1980s, crime degraded inner-city shopping strips throughout the nation. A 1999 *Initiative for a Competitive Inner City/Inc. Magazine* study found that nearly half of inner-city entrepreneurs believed perceptions of crime kept business out of the inner city, while around a quarter cited crime itself as a major consideration. . . . Academic, government, and business researchers have found that inner-city residents leave their neighborhoods for more than half of all purchases—a conclusion that affirmed reams of previous research. If crime falls, in other words, profit-seeking businesses will fill the void that exists in inner cities.

Consider what has happened in neighborhoods with fast-falling crime rates. . . .

Hunt's Point's Southern Boulevard–area shopping strip had a high vacancy rate (and several nearby vacant lots) during the early 1980s. Walking along the street, longtime resident and business owner Ray Colon stops frequently to point out a store that sat vacant for years as the neighborhood declined. Today, only a few storefronts lack tenants, and business leaders say they tend to rent quickly.

In the Hyde/Jackson Square commercial area—which covers a slightly larger area than Hyde Square proper—almost no vacancies exist, and a new supermarket and strip mall have greatly increased total commercial space. In Alphabet City, once desolate streetscapes have blossomed with boutiques and bistros, and the city has sold most of its (almost always abandoned) properties along Avenues A, B, C, and D to private developers. In Yucca Corridor, a strip mall that provided a hangout for homeless people and gang members has shut down to make way for a new community center. A new motel and a high-end boutique have opened up in recent years, and a large new drugstore opened in the spring of 2000.

Commercial streets have become safer and more pleasant in every neighborhood studied, and the business environment improves when falling crime rates extend the useful shopping day. As Mark Culliton, the director of the Upham's Corner Main Street [a city-funded community-improvement program], points out: "Certain kinds of businesses believed that they couldn't thrive along this strip where people would only shop in the daytime." Since 1994, the percentage of area residents who felt afraid to shop in the Upham's Corner area has declined by more than half. "If it had remained an open-air drug market, we simply couldn't have expanded," says Linda Heidinger, owner of a gift shop in Alphabet City. "In December when it's dark all the time, people aren't going to do Christmas shopping here when they can do it somewhere where they feel safer," she says.

Falling crime rates also mitigate entrepreneurs' fears. Nearly every merchant interviewed who operated through a period of high crime tells a story of being held up at gunpoint and feeling helpless against shoplifting. "[Getting held up] at gunpoint was a constant fear," says Hyde Square children's clothing store owner Tony Barros. "It was a fact of being a small businessman in this neighborhood." As James K. Stewart noted in *Policy Review*, the high cost of insurance and security systems can prevent businesses from ever opening in crime-ridden areas. . . .

Another effect of crime reduction is that law-abiding residents regain control of commercial sidewalks and other public places. Certain kinds of businesses, particularly liquor stores and bars, are often driven out, along with the criminal types they serve. . . .

With the improved atmosphere comes more competition —a boon for consumers, if not for individual businesses. For example, Barros, the Hyde Square clothier, says that his business remains below the $17,000-gross-sales-a-week level that he maintained when junkies taunted his customers. Of 23 retailers interviewed who worked through a period of high crime, not one said that falling crime rates played a key role in improving profits. On balance, however, falling crime rates serve to integrate inner-city shopping strips into the mainstream economy. Existing business owners do not always benefit, but the overall economy, residents, and shopping strips all thrive when crime goes down.

Home Improvement

Large reductions in crime also improve housing. Throughout the 1970s and 1980s, many buildings in the neighborhoods studied were destroyed. But reducing crime enables landlords to get returns high enough to stimulate increased investment in housing. In New York's Alphabet City and Hunt's Point, there has been several hundred million dollars in new housing construction and remodeling since the early 1980s. Investment in Hunt's Point by the two largest nonprofits, Banana Kelly and SEBCO, created over $600 million in new or remodeled housing during the 1980s and 1990s, while Alphabet City saw the drug-addicted squatters immortalized in the musical *Rent* evicted from its buildings as profit-making developers entered in large numbers.

Boston's Four Corners currently has $22 million worth of new residential construction in progress, with another $30 million or so in advanced planning stages. Upham's Corner has benefited from over $120 million in total new investment during the 1990s, slightly more private sector than public sector. In Hyde Square, requests for rehab permits have more than doubled since 1990, and several sizeable new buildings have gone up. Armory Revival has poured nearly

$10 million into Armory District construction and remodeling since it began operations. In Yucca, at least $5 million went toward refurbishment and redesign of dilapidated buildings. Units damaged during the 1994 Northridge earthquake were also quickly replaced. (Previous earthquake damage was repaired much more slowly.) Legal action by tenants' groups forced some landlords to perform basic repairs, while efforts to clean up other buildings continue. Requests for rehab permits also increased greatly.

In Garden Grove, California, Buena-Clinton has seen over $20 million in investment since the early 1980s—about half of it private (most of the money was spent in the early to mid 1980s, so the improvements would cost far more today). In 1983, all but three buildings in the area were substandard; today, almost none are. Stewart Drive, the smallest and newest neighborhood studied, benefited from $20 million in investment—almost all of it through tax-exempt bonds.

Developers point out that the relationship between housing improvement and crime reduction is quite complex. On one hand, working, law-abiding tenants won't move into neighborhoods where crime rates are horrific. On the other hand, the first stages of remodeling tend to bring in "pioneers" who brave high crime in return for freshly remodeled living spaces. Housing investment in the neighborhoods I visited began before the drop in crime, but without the improved environment the new investments could not have been sustained. Edward Kuo, through his company Golden Remco, remodeled apartments in Buena-Clinton before crime began to fall, but saw them trashed. "Banks found out that we knew how to handle money and they made us a sort of Community Reinvestment Act poster child," says Armory Revival general partner Le Baron Preston, "[but] if everything had gotten destroyed . . . eventually, the money would have dried up.". . .

Civil Society's Rebirth

In neighborhoods around the country, community organizations provide more services when crime falls. Safer neighborhoods enable residents to spend more time participating in community activities and allow community activists to focus on issues other than crime. In addition, people with middle-class values find their position strengthened when crime rates fall.

Less crime means safer evening hours and, as a result, more time for activities ranging from summer camps to sewing classes. Representatives of community organizations in neighborhoods with significant declines in crime all said that they now offer more activities in the evenings. In Hunt's Point, the Casita Maria settlement house, which closed at 7:00 P.M. most nights before crime rates began to fall, now stays open until 1:00 A.M. on weeknights. "It used to be that we couldn't fill a lot of programs in the winter because people were just too scared," says Casita Maria director Martha Rivera. "Today, we have waiting lists for ESL classes, basketball leagues, sewing classes, whatever." Rivera estimates that enrollment in the center's programs has more than doubled since New York City's crime rate began its steep decline in 1992.

In Garden Grove, the Boys and Girls Club and landlord Golden Remco have begun to offer classes in Buena-Clinton (virtually no community programs existed before), while the landlord-sponsored "Uth Force" tutoring program has increased high-school graduation rates along Stewart Drive. "As best as we know, not a single Hispanic kid in the neighborhood graduated from high school until five years ago," says neighborhood leader and property owner Vincent Vander Burgh. The numbers tell the story of Uth Force's success. In 1996, two area students finished high school; five did in 1997 and eight in 1998; 14 finished in 1999, and about the same number graduated in 2000. When the program first started, however, even getting students into the homework center proved a considerable challenge: Nobody wanted to come out at night. Now, Golden Remco's homework help center in Buena-Clinton stays open late nearly every school night—something manager Betty Chu says would have been impossible 15 years ago. Likewise, Buena-Clinton has gained a roller-hockey rink on the site of an apartment building once ruled by drug lords. . . .

Reducing crime also gives neighborhood activists more time to pay attention to their community's social needs. In its days as the Four Corners Public Safety Action Project, the Greater Four Corners Action Coalition dealt only with crime. Now the Coalition does everything from providing summer programs for children to attracting developers. "If you're worrying about crime all the time, then you can't really do much else," explains director Marvin Martin. Other community leaders echoed Martin's sentiments. "Once you've gotten crime down a little, you can move organizing efforts on to other topics—like city services, voter registration, parks, housing," says Jeanne DuBois, Executive Director of the Dorchester Bay Economic Development Corporation in Upham's Corner. In Dorchester, voter registration has boomed, while Reverend Eugene Rivers's organization has more than tripled the number of people it serves in Four Corners. Across town, the Hyde Square Task Force deals with about 150 youths a year through new summer camps and educational programs. When crime declines, government officials also have more time. "Five years ago, nearly all of our priorities would have had something to do with crime," says John Robert, the Community Board District Manager for the Hunt's Point area. "Now we can focus on parks."

Reducing crime also improves the credibility of the values of decency and hard work, and reduces the influence of what sociologist Elijah Anderson calls the "Code of the Street." As Anderson explains in his 1999 book by that name:

> Simply living in [a crime-ridden, downtrodden neighborhood] places young people at special risk of falling victim to aggressive behavior . . . street culture has evolved into a "code of the street" which amounts to informal rules governing interpersonal behavior, particularly violence.

As Anderson explains, even those who accept "decent" middle-class values need to know the Code of the Street in a neighborhood where violence represents a fact of daily life. . . .

When crime declines, however, community leaders and, more importantly, ordinary residents, feel far more free to assert their values. "A lot of it was a matter of getting into a strong enough position," says Eugene Rivers, who spearheaded Boston's area-wide 10 Point Coalition of black churches. "It sometimes seemed like we were only making a little bit of progress but, eventually, the walls began to come down." Mark Van Noppen tells a similar story about Armory Revival's work. "At first, we would always have to put up with these street punks and almost had to go to war with them," he says. "After a while, things changed." Ordinary residents also feel better. "When you have lots of people trashing their homes and doing drugs, it's hard to think that you'll have any place to work from," says Providence's Anne Hill. "Once you reach a certain point, it's a lot easier to take good care of your neighborhood."

A Conservative Social Policy

At least since the 1960s, a great many social scientists have thought that alleviating poverty will alleviate crime. In the early twenty-first century, this thesis stands on shaky ground. Some social programs, particularly those that work with children and inculcate moral values, probably do help reduce crime. But the latest wave of evidence shows that the best way to restore communities and lessen poverty is to reduce crime itself, not the supposed "root causes" of crime. The best-conceived and best-funded programs, public or private, will do little good in a dangerous environment. Alternatively, when falling crime rates bring commercial strips back to life, improve housing, help residents feel safe at night, and strengthen a community's stabilizing moral forces, it becomes possible to integrate even the most troubled areas into the American mainstream. So far the evidence looks good, and it is fair to say that crime-reduction ranks with welfare reform as the greatest social policy triumph of the past decade.

"The aggression-enhancing effect of exposure to television is chronic, extending into later adolescence and adulthood."

Media Violence Causes Violent Crime

Daphne Lavers

In the viewpoint that follows, Daphne Lavers argues that since their inception, movies and television have offered viewers increasingly violent fare, and she notes that the increase in media violence coincides with an overall increase in rates of violent crime. Lavers cites research showing that repeated exposure to media violence desensitizes viewers to violence and conditions them to associate violence with pleasure. In the most extreme cases, violent films have caused viewers to copy the murders portrayed on-screen. Lavers is a Toronto-based freelance journalist specializing in science, technology, and broadcasting issues.

As you read, consider the following questions:

1. What percent increase in television violence did the Parents Television Council report in its 2000–2001 study, as compared to its 1998–1999 study, as cited by the author?
2. What is the difference between operant and classical conditioning, according to psychologist David Grossman?
3. What are some of the movies that Lavers says have incited viewers to copy the murders committed in them?

Daphne Lavers, "Media Violence: Ugly and Getting Uglier," *World & I*, vol. 17, March 2002, p. 68. Copyright © 2002 by News World Communications, Inc. Reproduced by permission.

Murder rates doubled 10 to 15 years after the introduction of television in the United States, Canada, and virtually every country where "free" television was launched—truly a troubling anecdote.

In the last 10 years, violent female role models have emerged on movie and television screens. In the same decade, the violent crime rate has risen 93 percent among females compared to 35 percent for males, and the largest growing portion of the prison population is violent female inmates—another disturbing anecdote.

More than five decades after television's advent, its early promise "has been erased by the rapid degeneration of televised programming content," according to the Los Angeles–based Parents Television Council (PTC), which lobbies for more wholesome family TV fare.

Every new television season ramps up the violence, escalates sexual content, and increases questions about the purpose of this powerful teaching and entertainment device. In many families, media have replaced teachers and parents as educators, role models, and the primary sources of information about the world, according to a November [2001] report by the American Academy of Pediatrics (AAP). The warnings are mostly ignored, as industry debate focuses on technological tools that "rate" programs according to their violence and sexual content.

The general sense that film and television have increased the "raunch" factor in recent years has been quantified by the PTC in a study from the 2000–2001 television season.

"Family Hour" No More

The Sour Family Hour, a report by the PTC, showed "huge increases in coarse language (up 78 percent)" compared to the last study in 1998–99. (It equated coarse language with "verbal violence," seeing it as the starting point of the violence continuum.) Television violence was up a whopping 70 percent in the two years since the previous study, and "some of the sexual content fell into subcategories covering topics which a generation ago would seldom have seen the light of day in 10 P.M. programming, let alone 8 P.M. fare, [including] homosexuality, oral sex, pornography, masturbation, genitalia, and so-called

38

kinky practices, such as phone sex, group sex, and bondage."

Upset, the PTC wrote an open letter to the heads of the major television networks asking for the reinstatement of the "family hour" between 8 and 9 P.M. The organization also launched a campaign to "publicly shame those advertisers who market and sponsor the violence, sexual raunch, and vulgarity to our nation's children," said PTC President L. Brent Bozell. "We will name names, and often. It saddens and frustrates me no end that it has gotten to this point—publicly shaming adults for marketing trash to 10 million children every night."

Pushing such "trash" on children was the focus of a Federal Trade Commission (FTC) report in 2000 entitled *Marketing Violent Entertainment to Children: A Review of Self-Regulation and Industry Practices in the Motion Picture, Music Recording, and Electronic Game Industries*. Prompted by the Columbine High School massacre, it found that the entertainment industries routinely and illegitimately target-marketed violent entertainment directly to adolescents and preadolescents and then denied doing so.

In April 2001, the FTC reported some improvement in the movie and video game industries, notably in limiting advertising to teens and in providing "rating information."

In November 2001, the AAP reported that children between 2 and 18 years of age spend 6.5 to 8 hours a day with media, including television, videotapes, movies, and video games, more time than on any other activity except sleeping. By age 18, the average young person has seen 200,000 acts of violence on television alone. The report noted that, of 10,000 hours of broadcast programming reviewed by the National Television Violence Study, 61 percent portrayed interpersonal violence, much of it in an entertaining or glamorized manner. The highest proportion of violence was in children's programs; of all animated films produced in the United States between 1937 and 1999, 100 percent portrayed violence.

"Every year, the media use ever greater quantities of violence to hook their audience," said retired U.S. Army lieutenant colonel and media researcher Dave Grossman. "Why did the alcohol and tobacco industries want so desperately to continue to sell their products to children? Because the addictive process is so much more powerful if we can start when they're children. . . . [In visual imagery], the violence is the addictive substance; it is the nicotine in the cigarette, the alcohol in the beer."

The Psychology of Addiction

Grossman, a psychologist who studied and taught at West Point, researched how to overcome natural and instinctive barriers to killing, a task essential for the armed forces. He developed expertise in his own specialty, "killology," the science, psychology, and physiology of killing, and he has transferred that expertise to civilian life and the study of the media.

He has found that the psychological tools of repetition, desensitization, and escalation, combined with the instinct for survival, all contribute to a soldier's—or a child's—capacity for violence.

Repetition is a psychological technique to reduce or eliminate phobias by increasing exposure, which increases tolerance levels—the same paradigm as addiction. The practice is also the foundation of the advertising industry: More "exposures" equal more familiarity and increased comfort levels. Repetition of violence does the same through the process of desensitization.

"Over time, when desensitization works, the phobic response [against violence] becomes less and less intense," said Joanne Cantor, professor of communications at the University of Wisconsin, in an August 2000 speech before the American Psychology Association. "Exposure to media violence, particularly that which entails bitter hostilities or the graphic display of injuries, initially induces an intense emotional reaction in viewers. Over time and with repeated exposure, however, many viewers exhibit decreasing emotional responses to the depiction of violence and injury."

That decreasing response necessitates an escalation of video violence—increasing the dose, as it were—to maintain a reaction.

"People get jaded very quickly," said Neal Gabler, author and senior fellow at the Lear Center, a project of the University of Southern California's Annenberg School of Communication. "I compare popular culture to a drug. In popular culture, there is always a ratcheting mechanism. Once you've had

The Media Is Spreading a Virus of Violence

The per capita murder rate doubled in this country between 1957—when the FBI started keeping track of the data—and 1992. A fuller picture of the problem, however, is indicated by the rate people are attempting to kill one another—the aggravated assault rate. That rate in America has gone from around 60 per 100,000 in 1957 to over 440 per 100,000 by the middle of this decade. . . .

The crime rate is still at a phenomenally high level, and this is true worldwide. In Canada, according to their Center for Justice, per capita assaults increased almost fivefold between 1964 and 1993, attempted murder increased nearly seven-fold, and murders doubled. Similar trends can be seen in other countries in the per capita violent crime rates reported to Interpol between 1977 and 1993. In Australia and New Zealand, the assault rate increased approximately fourfold, and the murder rate nearly doubled in both nations. The assault rate tripled in Sweden, and approximately doubled in Belgium, Denmark, England-Wales, France, Hungary, Netherlands, and Scotland, while all these nations had an associated (but smaller) increase in murder.

This virus of violence is occurring worldwide. The explanation for it has to be some new factor that is occurring in all of these countries. There are many factors involved, and none should be discounted: for example, the prevalence of guns in our society. But violence is rising in many nations with draconian gun laws. And though we should never downplay child abuse, poverty, or racism, there is only one new variable present in each of these countries, bearing the exact same fruit: media violence presented as entertainment for children.

David Grossman, "Trained to Kill," *Christianity Today*, August 10, 1998.

---

this experience, this sensation, you want more; once you've had that, you reach a plateau and you want more." That's exactly what the creators of violent TV programs, films, and music aim to provide.

The Psychology of Conditioning

Once desensitization has begun, whether in viewers, addicts, or soldiers, conditioning—both operant and classical—reinforces that learned behavior.

"Operant conditioning teaches you to kill, but classical conditioning is a subtle but powerful mechanism that teaches you to like it," said Grossman.

Operant conditioning is the powerful, repetitive, stimulus-response training mechanism by which reactions are trained into automatic response, like a police officer on a firing range or a pilot in a flight simulator. Video games, some based on movies and television series, program exactly the same automatic, conditioned response and increasing skill level in children, often in marksmanship.

In fact, law enforcement agencies use the Firearms Training Simulator, more or less identical to the ultraviolent video game Time Crisis, said Toronto media activist Valerie Smith in her Media Violence 101 primer. The U.S. Army trains with the Multipurpose Arcade Combat Simulator, based on a modified Super Nintendo.

Classical conditioning associates a stimulus with some pleasurable response, developed in the Pavlovian experiments with dogs in which food was associated with an audio cue. Television connects visual media program content with advertising content.

"Our children watch vivid pictures of human suffering and death, and they learn to associate it with their favorite soft drink and candy bar or their girlfriend's perfume," said Grossman. "All the time in movie theaters when there is bloody violence, the young people laugh and cheer and keep right on eating popcorn and drinking soda. We have raised a generation of barbarians who have learned to associate violence with pleasure, like the Romans cheering and snacking as the Christians were slaughtered in the Coliseum."

The doubling of the murder rate following the introduction of television was discovered through an epidemiological study of murder by Brandon Centerwall, a professor of psychiatry and behavioral sciences at the University of Washington.

"All Canadian and U.S. studies of the effect of prolonged childhood exposure to television (two years or more) demonstrate a positive relationship between earlier exposure and later physical aggressiveness," Centerwall wrote in the *Journal of the American Medical Association.* "The critical period of exposure to television is preadolescent childhood. . . . The aggression-enhancing effect of exposure to television is chronic, extending into later adolescence and adulthood."

The phenomenon of killers committing replica homicides learned through murderous teaching tools from movies and television has been linked to *Natural Born Killers, Reservoir Dogs, Child's Play 3*, World Wrestling Federation, and *The Basketball Diaries*. The movie *Scream*, in which a slasher-murderer draped in black dons a mask inspired by Edvard Munch's painting *The Scream*, continues to inspire replica murders both in North America and Europe. The same month that the AAP released its policy on media violence [in 2001], a 24-year-old Belgian with no criminal record and no history of psychiatric problems dressed himself in a long black tunic, donned a *Scream* mask, and stabbed a 15-year-old schoolgirl 30 times. He told police the murder was premeditated and motivated by the *Scream* trilogy.

While most film and television people deny any responsibility for the increase in crime and violence, one exception is veteran film director Robert Altman, who blamed Hollywood for recent terrorism attacks. Altman, director of *M*A*S*H**, told the British Broadcasting Corporation last October [2001] that violent action films with big explosions, usually targeted at young men, amount to training films. He observed that "nobody would have thought to commit an atrocity like that unless they'd seen it in a movie."

While young men are the target audience, young women are most often the victims, whether in television series or serial-killer glorification movies. In her media violence primer, activist Smith observed that "the most extreme form of film violence, the splatter or slasher genre, was launched in 1963." This form of entertainment features people, primarily teenage girls and young women, being tortured, dismembered, disemboweled, and beheaded with various construction tools: chainsaws, tool guns, drills, jigsaws. The violence almost always takes place while the victims are naked or wearing skimpy lingerie.

Former FBI agent Robert Ressler and forensic psychiatrist Park Elliot Dietz, both experts on serial murder, believe these films have helped fuel the increase in serial killing, because of the explicit linking of sex with torture and murder in films targeted at a teenage audience.

Dietz put it this way: "If a mad scientist wanted to find a

way to raise a generation of sexual sadists in America, he could hardly do better at our present state of knowledge than to try to expose a generation of teenage boys to films showing women mutilated in the midst of a sexy scene."

The Technology "Fix"

Horror over television's content has prompted the creation of two technology fixes, both developed by Canadians for the North American market.

The V-chip, widely available in new TV sets and some cable set-top boxes, combines hardware and software to block programming according to rating codes and content categories. Developed by Canadian engineering professor Tim Collings, the V-chip uses the controversial national ratings system for television and televised movie programs.

CC+ is a hardware and software technology that blocks swearwords. It was developed by Alberta forklift driver and mother of four Diane LaPierre, who was appalled when one of her sons began learning how to spell swearwords from the captions on PG-13 television programs. CC+ works with the V-chip video technology, can be incorporated into new television sets, and is also available as a stand-alone black box.

Interestingly, new research has indicated a curious twist to the ratcheting up of visual violent imagery. In a research project released [in 2001], a study from the University of Iowa led by psychology professor Brad Bushman revealed that memory of TV commercials is lower if the programs they were seen with had violent and sexual content.

In a research study involving 324 men and women age 18–54, participants remembered advertising 39 percent better if seen within programs of neutral, rather than violent and sexual, content.

"Violence and sex impaired memory for males and females of all ages and for people who liked and did not like to watch televised violence and sex," Bushman said. "The sex and violence register much more strongly than the messages the advertisers are hoping to deliver."

It's ironic: Sex and violence designed to sell soap, soft drinks, and cars seem to sell—surprise!—mostly more sex and violence.

"Real love, real money, real political events and real-life . . . all shape kids' . . . behavior more powerfully than any entertainment products."

The Role of Media Violence in Violent Crime Has Been Exaggerated

Maggie Cutler

Maggie Cutler argues in the following viewpoint that, despite thousands of studies on the effects of media violence, the research has produced no clear answers. The author maintains that it is almost impossible to separate media violence from all the other factors that can influence violent behavior. One point that most researchers agree on, Cutler notes, is that real-life experiences are far more important than media violence in determining whether children commit violence. She concludes that leaders concerned about youth violence should focus on the real violence occurring in America and around the world rather than on movies, television, and video games. Cutler is the author of a Nerve.com biweekly column entitled "The Secret Life of Kitty Lyons," which satirizes the confusion between politics, media, and sex in American culture.

As you read, consider the following questions:

1. In addition to media violence, what factors does the American Psychology Association say are risk factors for youth violence, according to Cutler?
2. In the author's view, what was the main finding of the Stanford study headed by researcher Thomas Robinson?
3. What is the "rule of the real," as defined by the author?

Will girls imitate the new, kickass heroines in the Japanese anime *Cardcaptors?* Will the impressionable 12-year-olds exposed to trailers for MGM's *Disturbing Behavior* forever after associate good teen behavior with lobotomies? Did Nine Inch Nails and the video game *Doom* inspire the Trenchcoat Mafia's bloodbath at Columbine?[1] Thousands of studies have been done to try to answer variants of the question: Does media violence lead to real-life violence, making children more antisocial and aggressive?

Inconclusive Research

Like most complex issues, discussions about the impact of media violence on children suffer from that commonest of media problems: fudge. Almost any simple statement on the subject obscures the complexity of the facts, half-facts and "results suggest" findings of the past forty years. The right-wing Parents Television Council, for example, announces that the per-hour rate in the United States of sexual and violent material and coarse language combined almost tripled from 1989 to 1999. But while PTC president Brent Bozell castigates the media for lowering standards of acceptable speech and behavior, he doesn't mention that in the final years of this avalanche of dreck the juvenile crime rate dropped more than 30 percent. Or, again, in August 1999 the Senate Judiciary Committee, headed by Orrin Hatch, reported confidently that "Television alone is responsible for 10 percent of youth violence." Given the overall juvenile crime count in 1997, the report implied, some 250 murders and 12,100 other violent crimes would not have been committed if it weren't for the likes of *Batman Beyond.*

But this, of course, is deeply misleading. One of the reasons so many media violence studies have been done is that the phenomenon may be too complex to study conclusively. There's no way, after all, to lock two clones in a black box, feed them different TV, movie and video-game diets and open the box years later to determine that, yes, it was definitely those Bruce Lee epics that turned clone A into Jesse

1. Students known as the Trenchcoat Mafia opened fire at Columbine High School in Littleton, Colorado, on April 20, 1999.

Ventura, while clone B's exposure to the movie *Babe* produced a Pee Wee Herman.

It has been hard, in other words, for media violence studies to shake the ambiguity of correlations. Several studies have shown that violent boys tend to watch more TV, choose more violent content and get more enjoyment out of it. But the studies admittedly can't show exactly how or why that happens. Do temperamentally violent kids seek out shows that express feelings they already have, or are they in it for the adrenaline boost? Do the sort of parents who let kids pig out on gore tend to do more than their share of other hurtful things that encourage violent behavior? To what extent is violent media producing little Johnny's aggression—or inspiring it, making it appear glamorous, righteous, acceptably gratuitous, fun or "normal"—and to what extent is it merely satisfying little Johnny's greater-than-average longings for the mayhem, vengeance, superhuman power and sweet revenge that most people, at times, secretly crave?

One of Many Risk Factors

According to James Garbarino, author of *Lost Boys: Why Our Sons Turn Violent and How We Can Save Them*, it makes no sense to talk about violent media as a direct cause of youth violence. Rather, he says, "it depends": Media violence is a risk factor that, working in concert with others, can exacerbate bad behavior.

Like Orrin Hatch's committee, Garbarino estimates the effect of violent media on juvenile violence at about 10 percent, but his ecology-of-violence formulation is far less tidy than the Hatch committee's pop-psych model. Garbarino himself reports in an e-mail that he would like to see media violence treated as a public health problem—dammed at its Hollywood source the way sewage treatment plants "reduce the problem of cholera." Nevertheless, his ecology model of how juvenile violence emerges from complex, interacting factors means that hyperaggressive, "asset poor" kids are likely to be harmed by graphic depictions of violence, while balanced, "asset rich" kids are likely to remain unscathed. A few studies have even found that a "cathartic effect" of media violence makes some kids less aggressive. This wide range of individual variance makes policy prescriptions a tricky matter.

The American Psychological Association's Commission on Violence and Youth (1994) mentions violent media as only one among many factors in juvenile violence. It stresses that inborn temperament, early parental abuse or neglect, poverty, cognitive impairment, plus a deficiency of corrective influences or role models in various combinations will put a child at greater risk for violence, both as perpetrator and as victim. The APA found that many damaged kids' lives can be salvaged with early intervention. By the age of 8, these at-risk kids can be identified. Once identified they can be taught skills that enable them to resolve conflicts peacefully. The APA adds that parental guidance along with reducing kids' exposure to graphic violence can help keep them out of the correctional system. But for the kids most at risk, reducing representational violence is obviously no cure. So this past fall [2000], when Senators John McCain and Joseph Lieberman ordered the entertainment industry to stop advertising its nastier products to young children or else face (shudder) regulation, it was fair of media critics to castigate them for exploiting the media violence problem for its bipartisan glow rather than attempting to find the least coercive, most effective ways of keeping children safe and sane.

Perhaps the biggest problem in mitigating the effect of media violence on children is that it's hard to nail down just what "violent media" means to actual kids. As with adult pornography, we all think we know what it is until we have to define it. That's because kids not only process content differently depending on their temperament, background and circumstances, they seem to process it differently at different ages, too.

A series of often-cited studies known as Winick and Winick (1979) charted distinct stages in media processing abilities. Fairly early, from about 6 until about 10, most—but not all—kids are learning to deal with media much as adults do: interactively rather than passively. In her 1985 book, *Watching Dallas: Soap Opera and the Melodramatic Imagination*, Ien Ang of the University of Western Sydney in Australia showed that different adult viewers rewrote the "messages" of shows to suit their own views. So a wise little girl whose parents discuss media with her might enjoy Wrestlemania as an amusing guide to crazy-guys-to-avoid, while an angry, abandoned, slow-witted child is more likely to enter its world of insult and injury with uncritical awe.

A Lack of Evidence

Since this study will never be performed, critics of media violence are reduced to distorting the evidence or relying on impressionistic arguments. Children are constantly bombarded by violent images, they say, and it defies common sense to claim they're not affected.

The issue, of course, is not whether they're affected but how they're affected. And if some kids are so depraved that violent TV shows can turn them into criminals, getting rid of the shows is not the answer.

Jacob Sullum, "Missing Link," *Reason*, January 23, 2001.

At first blush, measures like content labeling would seem to make more sense for the 2-to-6 set because young kids do get confused about reality, fantasy, information and advertising. But again, what constitutes "violent" content isn't always obvious. The Winicks found that young children whose parents fought a lot responded with more distress to representations of people yelling and screaming—because it seemed real—than to blatant violence for which they had no frame of reference. Should there be a label for "loud and emotional"? And if so, should we slap it on *La Boheme?*

Because representational violence is so hard to define, the . . . Stanford media effects studies, which focused on third and fourth graders, ducked the problem. The study team, headed by Thomas Robinson, simply worked with teachers, parents and kids to help children lower their overall media use voluntarily. As a result of the six-month program, which involved classroom instruction, parental support and peer pressure, kids used media about 30 percent less than usual. And, they found, verbal and physical aggression levels subsequently dropped 25 percent on average. These numbers are being taken especially seriously because they were established "in the field" rather than in the lab, so that the verbal and physical aggression measured was actual, not simulated by, say, asking a child to kick or insult a doll. As media violence studies predicted, the more aggressive kids were to begin with, the more their behavior improved when they consumed less of whatever it was they normally consumed.

Although the Stanford study—perhaps to stay popular with granters—is being promoted as a study on media violence, it is really a study of media overuse, self-awareness and the rewards of self-discipline. Its clearest finding wasn't that media violence is always harmful but that too much mediated experience seems to impair children's ability to interact well with other people. Follow-up studies at Stanford will show whether the remarkable benefits of its media reduction program last over a longer period. If they do, such classes may be a helpful addition to school curriculums in conjunction, perhaps, with courses in conflict resolution. But in any case, its results demonstrate less the effects of specific content than what could be called "the rule of the real."

Real Life Has More Impact than Fantasy Violence

The rule of the real says that however strong media influences may be, real life is stronger. Real love, real money, real political events and real-life, unmediated interpersonal experience all shape kids' lives, minds and behavior more powerfully than any entertainment products. Even media seen or understood as real—news, documentaries, interviews—will have more impact than that which a kid knows is make-believe. As the Winicks found, kids understand early that cartoon violence is a joke, not a model. Even wrestling, once kids figure out that it's staged, gets processed differently from, say, a schoolyard beating.

Without belittling the importance of media research, it's time that the rule of the real governed policy as well. After all, boys whose dads do hard time tend to end up in jail, while boys who see *Fight Club* tend to end up in film clubs; it's more likely that the Santana High killer[2] decided to shoot up his school after seeing the anniversary coverage of Columbine

2. On March 5, 2001, a 15-year-old killed 2 students and wounded 13 others at a high school outside San Diego.

than because he watched *The Mummy*. Abused young women don't kill their battering husbands because they grew up watching *Charlie's Angels*, and teens who hear no criticism of the Gulf War tend to want another. Given limited energies and resources, if our politicians really wanted to reduce youth violence, they would push to reform prison policies, provide supervised after-school activities for teens and get early, comprehensive help to high-risk children. As a community, we would do better to challenge the corporate conglomeration of news outlets than to legislate the jugs 'n' jugular quotient in *Tomb Raider*, its labeling or ad placements—and this is true even though the stuff kids like is often quite nasty, and even though the better part of the scientific establishment now agrees that such excitements are less than benign. But setting priorities like these is hard because, while the real may rule children's lives as it rules our own, it's much more fun to imagine controlling their dreams.

*"There is an indisputable correlation
between drug use and crime."*

Drug Abuse Causes Crime

Dan P. Alsobrooks

Dan P. Alsobrooks is a district attorney general for the 23rd
Judicial District in Tennessee, and president of the National
District Attorneys Association in Virginia. In the viewpoint
that follows, he argues that drug use causes crime. To obtain
money to support their habit, writes Alsobrooks, drug users
steal and murder. He notes that a large proportion of federal
prison inmates were under the influence of drugs when they
committed their crimes. Alsobrooks criticizes supporters of
drug legalization who argue that drug law penalties should
be reduced or that drug abuse is a victimless crime. He maintains that most people in prisons for drug offenses are there
for dealing drugs, not simply possessing them, and he cites
statistics on how drug abuse costs society. Alsobrooks warns
that while America's drug policy has been effective in reducing drug abuse, growing complacency about drugs could
cause rates of drug abuse—and rates of crime—to once again
increase.

As you read, consider the following questions:
1. What percentage of New York State inmates were
   incarcerated for selling drugs or intent to sell drugs,
   according to the author?
2. What percentage of state and federal inmates does
   Alsobrooks say reported being under the influence of
   drugs at the time they committed murder, as of 2000?
3. How many fewer people does the author say use drugs
   today as compared to in the late 1970s?

Dan P. Alsobrooks, "Waging a Battle Against Myths," *Corrections Today*, vol. 64,
December 2002, p. 86. Copyright © 2002 by American Correctional Association,
Inc. Reproduced by permission.

rosecutors know through experience that the majority of crimes in communities are drug-related. This is an indisputable fact, backed by incontrovertible evidence, including prosecutors' bulging caseloads. Those who seek to decriminalize drug use ignore the facts and the evidence, relying on myths to mislead the public and advance their cause.

The crimes related to substance abuse range far beyond drug possession. They run the gamut from environmental pollution to murder. Crimes include gang wars to control drug markets; methamphetamine manufacturing sites that are a biohazard; and deaths caused by drug-impaired drivers. The list goes on.

Supporters of Drug Legalization Are Misguided

Propositions, proposals and legislation to legalize or decriminalize controlled substances are springing up around the country. The drug legalization movement is well-funded and highly adept at manipulating the media. Unless law enforcement speaks out more forcefully, our communities will find themselves facing an onslaught of violence and death directly attributable to the use of dangerous and poisonous drugs that have previously been controlled. We face a well-financed opposition with a well-organized political machine that can outspend us state by state and referendum by referendum. Operating under umbrella groups, the opposition uses a legislative strategy akin to the death of a thousand cuts. Those who want to legalize drugs advance their position, issue by issue, winning by incremental victories, while law enforcement officials often regard such victories as isolated losses.

For example, in one state, a legalization referendum misleads voters to believe that the issue is alleviating suffering for cancer patients. In another state, the issue is disguised as a legislative mandate to decriminalize certain types of drug use and provide treatment programs. And in a third state, legalization efforts are an attempt to limit asset forfeiture. Each such manipulation chips away at the foundation of law enforcement's efforts to fight substance abuse throughout the nation. With each such victory, those who would undermine law enforcement grow stronger and our communities become less safe.

More than 100 of these so-called and cleverly disguised drug policy "reforms" have been enacted in 40 states since 1996 and 41 were enacted in 2001 alone. There have been some successful efforts to reject some so-called reforms, most notably in Massachusetts and Oregon, but they remain in the minority. Those who would legalize drugs boast of their success in Nevada, where [in 2001], marijuana was decriminalized and where [in 2002], the issue on the ballot was actual legalization. [The initiative failed.] Their propaganda machine exulted that "voters in Florida, Michigan and Ohio will likely vote on sweeping 'treatment instead of incarceration' initiatives in November [2002]. The initiatives are similar to measures voters approved in Arizona (1996) and California (2002)."

More ominously, those who support the drug legalization effort brag that the American people are significantly changing their opinions on drug abuse and the criminal justice system and that this "shift in public opinion" will lead to a groundswell of support for their cause. On one of the proponents' Web sites, they boldly claim, "States are reigning in the excesses of the war on drugs regardless of what the federal government is doing. Since most drug arrests occur at the state level, state reforms are having a huge impact on the lives of millions of Americans. At the rate states are reforming their drug laws, the federal government may very soon find itself alone in supporting punitive and antiquated drug policies."

Battling the Myths

A major aspect of the public relations effort to bring about the state-by-state change rests on the continual repetition of myths. This, plus the American public's lack of understanding of the real dangers of substance abuse, provides those who support legalization with a sometimes-winning media campaign. Americans appear to be in serious denial about the problems associated with drugs: It is "someone else's child"; "something that will never hurt me"; or "someone else's life that will be jeopardized, not mine." Unless law enforcement officials counter such myths and convince America that these substances are not harmless, that the criminal justice system does not ruin people's lives, but rather, dangerous and addictive drugs do, they will continue to lose the fight and the legalization lobby's prophecies will come true.

One of the most popular myths regarding drugs is that jails are filled with people who are guilty only of possession for personal use. Law enforcement officials know that this is not true. The fact is that most individuals who are found in simple possession of drugs are placed in diversion and treatment programs and that this is not a new trend. Prosecutors and the courts have long recognized that prison cells should be reserved for the worst offenders and for those who refuse to rehabilitate and reform their dangerous conduct. Unfortunately, part of the basis for this myth is a practice of some prosecutors that should be explained or changed. Too often, offenders are sent to prison as the result of a plea agreement under which a charge of selling drugs is reduced to simple possession. Additionally, offenders may be incarcerated for possession with intent to distribute a controlled substance—a very different offense than possession for personal use. Further, many offenders who have been provided with rehabilitation opportunities and probation violate the conditions of their release and leave the courts no option but to incarcerate them.

According to a study published by the New York State Department of Corrections, of the 22,000 people in jail in New York for drug crimes, 87 percent were incarcerated for selling drugs or intent to sell drugs. Of the 12 percent incarcerated for possession, 76 percent were arrested for selling drugs and pleaded down their charges to possession. Additionally, the study found that most convicted first-time drug offenders end up on probation or in drug treatment rather than in jail. Statistics from Florida are similar. According to the Florida Department of Law Enforcement, of the 1,555 inmates in prison for drug possession on July 31, 2001, none were first-time offenders.

Each state has a similar story to tell and research must be conducted and data obtained that reflect the actual basis for incarceration. Likewise, prosecutors must understand that by pleading down cases, they are, in some instances, providing ammunition to their opponents. They need to tell their many success stories—of their drug courts [which treat, rather than incarcerate, minor drug offenders], their diversion and treatment programs, and their efforts at all stages in the criminal

"All Dopers Are Thieves"

As my fellow cops can tell you, drugs and crime go together like gum and sidewalks. . . .

The vast majority of criminals we arrest are drug users to one degree or another. There is a saying around here, "Not all thieves are dopers but all dopers are thieves." One local "fence" supplied drugs to an entire group of high schoolers by trading them their highs in return for guns, jewelry, and other goods the kids stole. . . .

A quick survey of my caseload reveals that about 85 percent of my current cases are drug related. The crimes range from burglary to assault to credit card fraud. One victim had her house ransacked, and within days her checks began showing up at stores throughout the county. She starting getting notices from check-clearing companies all over the country. The paperwork drove her crazy, not to mention ruining her credit.

Check forging is big business in the drug economy. Stolen blank checks are sold or traded for drugs with dealers, who then either resell them or send out their street whores to write them at stores. Many stores just swipe the check and let the purchase go through without checking ID.

A while back we had a series of purse snatchings done by a white male and his two white female crackhead prostitutes. They targeted elderly women, knocking them down then taking their purses. Before we had even finished writing up a crime report the young women would be at a grocery store or a large discount store passing their checks.

In addition to the crimes committed by drug users to obtain money for drugs, sometimes drugs themselves simply cause crime. More than four times as many murders are committed under the influence of drugs as are committed to get money to buy drugs, according to federal and state data. Many needless lesser offenses are committed by people while in a drugged condition.

I have arrested countless people, mostly teens, who have broken into homes, been involved in brawls, assaulted females, stolen cars, and committed similar offenses, only to hear the excuse that "I was so stoned/blasted/high I don't remember much of what happened." Many of the people I arrest say that if they weren't on drugs they would never have done what they did. And I believe them.

Ray Wisher, "Joint at the Hip," *American Enterprise*, June 2001.

justice system to provide substance abuse treatment. Prosecutors also must inform the public that without the threat of incarceration, habitual and addicted drug offenders will not enter or complete rehabilitation programs. This is very much in accord with former President Teddy Roosevelt's axiom of speaking softly but carrying a big stick—here, prosecutors' "stick" to ensure diversion program participation is the fear of going to jail.

The Victims of Drug Abuse

Another myth, popular with a culture that has advertising campaigns flouting the need to follow societal rules, is that drug abuse is a victimless crime. The use of illegal drugs is not victimless. Regretfully, nearly every family has been hurt by addiction. It has consequences that touch the lives of children and adults nationwide. The victims of drug abuse range from those physically harmed by drug-induced crimes to taxpayers footing the bill for drug treatment. In other words, every citizen is a victim, either directly or indirectly.

Drugs are illegal because they are harmful, both to immediate users and to others who become victimized by the effects of drugs on users. In 1999, there were 19,102 deaths from drug-induced causes (legal and illegal drugs). During that year, there were 168,763 cocaine-related emergency room episodes alone. The following year, the Substance Abuse and Mental Health Administration's Drug Abuse Warning Network reported that there were 601,563 drug-related episodes in hospital emergency rooms nationwide. Who is paying the bills for these cases? The numbers speak for themselves. Between 1992 and 1998, the overall cost of drug abuse to society increased at a rate of 5.9 percent annually. By 1998, victimless crime was costing society $143.4 billion each year for health-related expenses alone. This, however, does not include the emotional costs to those actually victimized by substance abuse: the battered spouses, victims of impaired drivers and victims of assault and rape. These costs are beyond calculation.

Drug Availability Increases Crime Rates

A third myth used to support legalization is that drug use does not impact crime rates. One must wonder whether the people who say this have ever spoken to the victim of an assailant high on drugs; to the parents of a child killed by an impaired driver; or to a nurse who sees babies born to drug-addicted mothers every day. It is well-known that crimes result from a variety of factors and often cannot be attributed solely to drug abuse. The connection between drug use and crime is difficult to quantify due to exaggeration or minimization by the offender, lack of prompt testing and inaccuracy of victims' descriptions of whether the offender used drugs. However, many of the criminal acts seen every day have their origins in drug use. The American public must be convinced of this.

The need to obtain money to feed a habit, the rage empowered by drugs, the protection or disruption of the drug marketplace—each has its role in the crime cycles surrounding drug use. There is an indisputable correlation between drug use and crime, and it is obvious that the combination of increased availability of drugs and a decrease in the stigma for drug use will result in an increase in crime. Although the number of drug-related homicides has decreased in recent years, murders related to narcotics rank as the fourth most documented murder circumstance of 24 possible categories. In 2000, the Uniform Crime Reporting Program of the FBI reported that 4.4 percent of the 12,943 homicides in which circumstances were known were narcotic-related. In 1998, 36 percent of convicted jail inmates were under the influence of drugs at the time of the offense. Drugs affect the user's judgment and behavior. In 1997, illicit drug users were 16 times more likely to be arrested for larceny or theft, 14 times more likely to be arrested for driving under the influence and more than nine times more likely to be arrested on assault charges.

During that same year, 29.4 percent of state and federal prison inmates reported being under the influence of drugs at the time they committed murder, 27.8 percent reported being under the influence of drugs at the time they committed robbery and 13.8 percent reported being under the influence at the time they committed assault. How much more proof is needed? Against these statistics, arguments that legalization will not impact crime rates do not hold up.

A final myth being advanced by legalization supporters is

that decriminalization will not increase drug use. This is a fatalistic kind of a "que sera, sera" argument: "whatever will be, will be." Decriminalizing drugs sends the dangerous message that drug abuse is not harmful. This, an obvious lie, ignores the fact that drug abuse claims the lives of 14,000 Americans annually and costs taxpayers nearly $70 billion. In conveying this message, society would be tacitly approving the use of drugs. If drugs were legalized and market forces prevailed, what, for example, would stop the marijuana industry from sponsoring commercials for children to see during Super Bowl halftime?

According to the 2001 Monitoring the Future Study, 73.3 percent of high school seniors had used alcohol within the past 12 months. During the same period, 37 percent had used marijuana. Arguably, the difference is attributed to the fact that alcohol is more readily available because it is legal for adults to purchase and consume. Conversely, the private industrial sector has repeatedly demonstrated that a tough, enforced drug policy sharply reduces sick days, on-the-job accidents and workers' compensation claims. Drugs, even legally used, are not harmless; nor are they cost-free to society.

The War on Drugs

America's drug policy is not, as the critics contend, a dismal failure and a wasted effort. The statistics prove otherwise. The problem has been law enforcement's failure to effectively report its successes, warn of the true risks of substance abuse and to fully involve an educated community.

Overall drug use is down 50 percent since the late 1970s, which translates into 9.3 million fewer people using illegal drugs. Cocaine use has decreased 75 percent during the past 15 years, which means that 4 million fewer people are using cocaine on a regular basis. Less than 5 percent of the population use illegal drugs of any kind. Moreover, in the past, legalization and decriminalization reforms have failed, leading to increased drug use and the accompanying increases in social problems, health costs and economic repercussions. The use of drugs has decreased markedly since it reached the high point in the late 1970s, but it is not low enough. Too many Americans use drugs and too many other Americans are becoming victims of those who use drugs.

Even more dangerous is the complacency among prosecutors. If they, and others in law enforcement, do not sustain their efforts to tell the American people the truth about substance abuse, society as a whole will suffer and statistics on drug-related crime will continue to rise, fall and rise again as each generation relearns the mistakes of the previous generation. Law enforcement officers are sworn to protect the public and they need to be consistent and successful in their efforts to educate and warn society of the dangers of drug abuse. To date, there has not been success in these efforts. For the sake of the nation's future, success must be realized.

"The 'war on drugs' . . . has affected all aspects of the criminal justice system."

The War on Drugs Exacerbates America's Crime Problem

The Sentencing Project

The Sentencing Project is a nonprofit organization that promotes reduced reliance on incarceration and increased use of more humane alternatives to deal with crime. In the following viewpoint the project maintains that harsh drug laws have resulted in the imprisonment of hundreds of thousands of men and women. This has strained the prison system and diverted law enforcement resources from fighting other types of crime, the organization asserts. The Sentencing Project maintains that the majority of those incarcerated for drug violations are not high-level drug dealers and have not committed a violent crime. In addition, the project contends that the war on drugs has worsened racial discrimination within the criminal justice system, since the majority of those imprisoned for drug offenses are black.

As you read, consider the following questions:

1. In 1999 what percentage of state prison inmates, and what percentage of federal prison inmates, were drug offenders, as stated in the viewpoint?
2. What percentage of imprisoned drug offenders are black, according to the Sentencing Commission?
3. What proportion of federal antidrug funds are devoted to law enforcement as opposed to prevention and treatment, according to the Sentencing Project?

The Sentencing Project, *Drug Policy and the Criminal Justice System*, www. sentencingproject.org, August 2001. Copyright © 2001 by The Sentencing Project. Reproduced by permission.

No issue has had more impact on the criminal justice system in the past two decades than national drug policy. The "war on drugs" that was declared in the early 1980s has been a primary contributor to the enormous growth of the prison system in the U.S. since that time and has affected all aspects of the criminal justice system. As a response to the problem of drug abuse, national drug policies have emphasized punishment over treatment and have had a disproportionate impact on low-income communities and minorities.

Drug Policies Have Increased Arrests and Prison Populations

Drug arrests have tripled since 1980. Responding to a perceived problem of high rates of drug abuse in the late 1970s, the Reagan administration and other political leaders officially launched a "war on drugs" policy in 1982. Within a few years, both funding for drug law enforcement and a political focus on the drug war had increased substantially. As a result, there was a surge of arrests for drug offenses in the 1980s. The total of 581,000 arrests in 1980 nearly tripled to a record high of 1,584,000 by 1997 and continues close to that level with 1,532,300 in 1999. In 1999, four of five (80.5%) drug arrests were for possession and one of five (19.5%) for sales. Overall, 40.5% of drug arrests were for marijuana offenses.

While rates of drug use were relatively high in 1979 just prior to the inception of the drug war, they had begun to decline even prior to the formal inception of the "war" several years later. This decline parallels similar reductions in smoking and consumption of high fat foods, as many Americans have become increasingly interested in leading a healthy lifestyle. The heightened level of drug arrests continued even as drug use further declined and then stabilized. Government household surveys of drug use indicate that 14.1% of the population were monthly drug users in 1979. This figure declined by more than half to 6.6% by 1991 and remained in that range throughout the 1990s. More than half (57%) of all persons who use drugs monthly use marijuana but no other drugs. Against this overall decline, the number of arrests continues at record levels.

Drug offenders represent a rising proportion of offenders in prison. As seen in the figure below, in 1980 there were 19,000 offenders in state prisons for drug offenses and 4,900 in federal prisons, representing 6% and 25% of all inmates respectively. By 1999, a more than twelve-fold increase in drug offenders in state prisons led to a total of 251,200, constituting 21% of the inmate population. Dramatic increases occurred in the federal system as well, as the number of drug offenders rose to 68,360 representing 57% of all inmates. As drug offenders swelled the nation's prisons, the proportion of prison space used to house violent offenders declined. In 1986, states were using 55% of their prison space for offenders convicted of a violent offense; by 1999, that proportion had declined to 48%.

Drug Offenders in State and Federal Prisons, 1980–1999

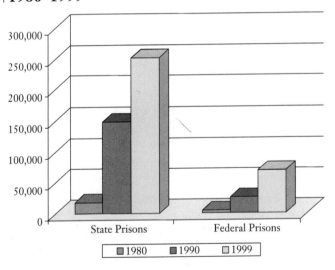

The Sentencing Project, *Drug Policy and the Criminal Justice System*, August 2001.

Harsher sentencing laws have contributed to the increased number of drug offenders in prison. Along with the stepped-up pace of arrests in the 1980s, legislatures throughout the country adopted harsher sentencing laws in regard to drug offenses. Today, every state and the federal system have some type of mandatory sentencing laws requiring imprisonment, most often used for drug offenses. These laws remove discretion from the sentencing judge to consider the range of factors pertaining to the individual and the offense that would normally be an integral aspect of the sentencing process.

Largely as a result of these laws, the chances of receiving a prison term after being arrested for a drug offense rose dramatically—by 447%—between just 1980 and 1992.

The prosecution of many drug offenders is discretionary and can be subject to either state or federal jurisdiction. In recent years there has been a dramatic increase in the number of drug prosecutions brought in federal court, a rise of 233% in the period of 1985–99. This has led to more offenders being brought under the scope of the mandatory minimum penalties adopted by Congress in 1986 and 1988, among the most severe in the nation. These laws require a mandatory five-year prison term for possessing as little as five grams of crack cocaine (the weight of two pennies).

In recent years there have been some modest signs of legislative bodies reconsidering the wisdom of mandatory sentencing laws. In 1998, the Michigan Legislature substantially scaled back a twenty-year-old law that mandated imprisonment of life without parole for distribution of 650 grams of cocaine or heroin. The penalty was the same as for first degree murder in Michigan and applied even to first offenders. After more than 200 offenders were sentenced under the law, changes were enacted that now permit parole consideration after fifteen years.

In 1994, Congress adopted a "safety valve" provision that applies to federal drug cases. Under this statute, judges are permitted to sentence offenders below the applicable mandatory minimum penalty (though not less than two years in prison) if the offender has a minimal prior record, there is no involvement in violence in the offense, and if the offender provides "substantial assistance" to the prosecution. Since the adoption of this provision, 25% of federal drug cases are now sentenced in this way, providing an indication of the degree to which low-level offenders are being prosecuted.

Many Drug Offenders Are Inappropriately Incarcerated

Drug offenders are now serving longer prison terms. In addition to resulting in the sentencing of greater numbers of drug offenders to prison, mandatory sentencing laws have also increased the average time served in prison for drug offenders since they eliminate the possibility of parole. In the federal system, for example, drug offenders released from prison in 1986 who had been sentenced before the adoption of mandatory sentences and sentencing guidelines had served an average of 22 months in prison. Offenders sentenced in 1999, after the adoption of mandatory sentences, were expected to serve almost three times that length, or 62 months in prison.

Most drug offenders in prison are not drug kingpins. A primary rationale provided for federal prosecution of high-level drug offenses is that the federal system is equipped with the level of resources necessary to handle these cases. One would therefore expect that federal drug cases on average should be composed of high-level offenders. Research conducted by the U.S. Sentencing Commission, though, documents that in 1992, only 11% of federal drug defendants consisted of high-level dealers, while 55% were either street-level dealers or mules, and 34% mid-level dealers.

A 1992 report by the Department of Justice reached similar conclusions, finding that 36% of all federal prison inmates serving drug sentences were low-level offenders. While there are no comprehensive data on drug offenders prosecuted in state courts, it is likely that they are even more disproportionately low-level offenders since high-level offenders have a greater likelihood of being prosecuted in federal court.

A substantial portion of prison inmates have a history of substance abuse. While approximately 450,000 inmates in prison and jail are currently incarcerated for a drug offense (possession or sale of drugs), additional numbers are incarcerated for drug-*related* offenses. These could include a burglary committed to obtain money to buy drugs or an assault committed under the influence of drugs. More than half (57%) of state prison inmates in 1997 had used drugs in the month prior to their arrest, and about one-sixth committed their offense in order to obtain money to buy drugs. Violent offenses were more likely to be committed by someone under the influence of alcohol (42%) than drugs (29%).

Prison inmates are less *likely to be receiving drug treatment.* Although there are a greater number of substance-abusing offenders in prison than in past years, the proportion of such inmates receiving treatment while in prison has declined. In state prisons, one in ten (9.7%) inmates in 1997 had participated in treatment since admission to prison, down from one in four (24.5%) inmates in 1991. Similar declines occurred in the federal prison system, with only 9.2% of inmates in 1997 receiving treatment, compared to 15.7% in 1991.

The War on Drugs and Race

Drug policies and enforcement have disproportionately affected African Americans. While African Americans use drugs on a regular basis at a slightly higher rate than other groups (7.7% current users compared to 6.6% for whites and 6.8% for Hispanics), their smaller numbers in the population results in their comprising 13% of monthly drug users. Whites represent 72% of users, Hispanics 11% and others 4%.

The impact of greater emphasis on law enforcement and incarceration of drug offenders has had a dramatic impact on the incarceration of African Americans as a result of three overlapping policy decisions: the concentration of drug law enforcement in inner city areas; harsher sentencing policies, particularly for crack cocaine; and, the drug war's emphasis on law enforcement at the expense of prevention and treatment. Given the shortage of treatment options in many inner city areas, drug abuse in these communities is more likely to receive attention as a criminal justice problem, rather than a social problem.

As a result, African Americans who use drugs are more likely to be arrested than other groups, and then to penetrate more deeply into the criminal justice system. While African Americans constitute 13% of the nation's monthly drug users, they represent 35% of those persons arrested for drug crime, 53% of drug convictions, and 58% of those in prison for drug offenses. Higher arrest rates of African Americans generally reflect a law enforcement emphasis on inner city areas, where drug sales are more likely to take place in open air drug markets and fewer treatment resources are available.

Once in the criminal justice system, African American drug offenders are often treated more harshly than other racial groups. The best documented area in which this takes place is in regard to sentencing for crack cocaine offenses. Crack cocaine and powder cocaine have the same chemical composition, but crack is marketed in less expensive quantities and so is more often used in low-income and minority communities. Under federal law, and similar statutes in some states, offenders convicted of crack cocaine offenses are punished more severely than those convicted of powder cocaine offenses. Thus, in federal court an offender selling five grams of crack cocaine receives the same five-year mandatory minimum sentence as does an offender selling five hundred grams of powder cocaine. As of 1999, 85% of all offenders sentenced in federal court for crack offenses were African American.

The Need for a Change in Drug Policy

Drug treatment is more cost-effective than mandatory sentencing. A series of studies in recent years have demonstrated that drug treatment—both within and outside the criminal justice system—is more cost-effective in controlling drug abuse and crime than continued expansion of the prison system. A RAND analysis of these issues concluded that whereas spending $1 million to expand the use of mandatory sentencing for drug offenders would reduce drug consumption nationally by 13 kilograms, spending the same sum on treatment would reduce consumption almost eight times as much, or 100 kilograms. Similarly, expanding the use of treatment was estimated to reduce drug-related crime up to 15 times as much as mandatory sentencing.

Studies of drug treatment in prisons have also concluded that inmates who receive treatment are significantly less likely to recidivate than those who do not. One of the oldest such programs is the Stay'n Out program in New York State, established in 1977 as a prison-based therapeutic community. Evaluations of the program have found that 27% of its male graduates are rearrested after parole, compared with 40% of inmates who received no treatment or only counseling.

Women's rearrest rates were generally lower than for men.

The war on drugs has distorted law enforcement priorities in fighting crime. Since there are no "cost-free" choices in public policy, the emphasis on drug enforcement since the early 1980s has created a set of unintended consequences for crime policy as well. These include:

- *Diverting law enforcement resources from other crime problems.* Increased law enforcement attention to low-level drug offenders inevitably results in fewer resources devoted to other types of offenses. Economists at Florida State University found that a 47% increase in drug arrests by Illinois law enforcement officers between 1984 and 1989 coincided with a 22.5% decline in arrests for drunk driving. They concluded that increased traffic fatalities could result from the more limited attention devoted to drunk driving.

- *Asset forfeiture laws threatening civil liberties and distorting priorities.* As a result of federal asset forfeiture legislation passed by Congress, both federal and local police agencies can seize any "drug-related" assets of suspected drug dealers and use any seized funds to augment law enforcement agency budgets even if the suspect is never charged with a crime. As of 1994, local police forces had received almost $1.4 billion in assets, while 80% of asset seizures failed to result in a criminal conviction. By depositing funds directly into law enforcement accounts, asset forfeiture laws create an incentive for police agencies to favor drug law enforcement over other categories of crimes.

- *Impact on women and children.* Women in prison are considerably more likely than men to have been convicted of a drug offense. As of 1998, 34% of women offenders had been convicted of a drug offense, compared to 20% of men, and two-thirds have children under 18. As a result of the federal welfare legislation of 1996, there is now a lifetime ban on the receipt of welfare for anyone convicted of a drug felony, unless a state chooses to opt out of this provision. As of 1999, half (24) the states are fully enforcing the provision, which means that drug offenders will have an even more difficult transition back into the community than ex-offenders generally. Eight states have chosen to opt out of the ban and another 18 have modified it, such as exempting persons convicted of possession offenses. The criminal penalties attached to drug use by pregnant women in some states present an additional problem for women by creating disincentives to seek treatment.

More rational drug policies could readily be implemented. A substantial body of research now exists that documents the injustices and inefficiencies of drug policies that emphasize enforcement and incarceration over prevention and treatment. The war on drugs has contributed substantially to a vastly expanded prison system and exacted a heavy toll on minority communities in particular. Despite advances in treatment and innovations such as drug courts, 30% of inmates sentenced to prison have been convicted of a drug offense.

Policymakers have the opportunity to effect a substantial shift in approach to the drug problem. The elements of such a change should include the following:

- *Shift funding priorities.* Since the 1980s, two-thirds of federal anti-drug funds have been devoted to law enforcement and just one-third to prevention and treatment. Although the federal drug budget is composed of various appropriations, a coordinated effort by the Administration and Congress could result in a shift toward a more pro-active and preventive strategy.

- *Repeal mandatory sentencing laws.* The legislative modifications to mandatory sentencing in Michigan and through the federal "safety valve" demonstrate that overly harsh sentencing laws can be altered without legislators suffering political consequences. Given that 25% of federal offenders are now sentenced under the safety valve, Congress should, at a minimum, examine the potential for expansion of that provision to additional offenders. At both the federal and state levels, legislators should reassess the wisdom and necessity of mandatory sentencing laws when other sentencing and treatment options exist.

- *Increase treatment options within the criminal justice system.* An increasing proportion of prison admissions in recent years consists of probation and parole violators, often as a result of drug use. More than one-third (37%) of offenders admitted to prison in 1998 consisted of such violators, double the rate (17.6%) in 1980. While political leaders in recent years have issued calls for mandatory drug testing of offenders under community supervision, in many jurisdictions treatment resources for this group are very inadequate.

Drug courts that divert defendants into treatment have expanded considerably in recent years, with more than 300 such courts now in operation. Their use could be expanded to additional jurisdictions as well as to an expanded group of defendants in many systems by eliminating unnecessary restrictions on eligibility.

- *Fund defense intervention services.* Defender offices often provide the first opportunity for criminal justice personnel to assess defendant needs. Far too many such offices lack the resources to prepare adequate assessment and service plans for their clients. State and county officials can fund enhanced defender services that can aid the court system in directing appropriate substance-abusing defendants into treatment services either as a diversion from the court system or as a component of a sentencing plan.

- *Approach drug abuse primarily as a community problem.* Although there are laudable programs within the criminal justice system for responding to problems of substance abuse, the criminal justice system was never designed as a social services agency. While substance abusers with adequate resources generally make use of private treatment providers to address their problems, low-income drug users are more likely to become involved in the criminal justice system due in part to the shortage of treatment options available to them. The public health model favored by middle class persons is one that could be extended to all communities given the political will to do so. Federal and state funding could be expanded to make treatment more widely available without the prerequisite of arrest and involvement in the criminal justice system.

Periodical Bibliography

The following articles have been selected to supplement the diverse views presented in this chapter.

Sasha Abramsky — "Did *Roe v. Wade* Abort Crime?" *American Prospect*, January 1, 2001.

David Boyum and Mark A.R. Kleiman — "Breaking the Drug-Crime Link," *Public Interest*, Summer 2003.

Business Week — "Does Abortion Lower the Crime Rate?" September 27, 1999.

Canada & the World — "Racial Tensions: Much of the Crime Among Immigrants Is Linked to Poverty," December 2002.

Louis Gesualdi — "Don't Blame Mom for Crime," *Humanist*, May/June 1998.

Dave Grossman — "Trained to Kill," *Christianity Today*, August 10, 1998.

Thomas L. Jipping — "Diagnosing the Cultural Virus," *World & I*, July 1999.

Michael D. Lemonick — "The Search for a Murder Gene," *Time*, January 20, 2003.

Kevin Merida and Richard Leiby — "When Death Imitates Art," *Washington Post*, April 22, 1999.

Richard Rhodes — "Hollow Claims About Fantasy Violence," *New York Times*, September 7, 2000.

USA Today — "Hot Weather Helps Crime to Grow," July 2000.

Ray Wisher — "Joint at the Hip," *American Enterprise*, June 2001.

Does Controlling Guns Control Crime?

Chapter Preface

According to health researcher Etienne Krug, the homicide rate in the United States is six times higher than that of other developed nations. And though the rate varies from year to year, according to the FBI, in the United States guns are used in about 70 percent of homicides. One of the main tenets of America's gun control movement is that reducing the availability of guns would reduce crime.

Of course, progun groups such as the National Rifle Association reject this claim. On the contrary, they argue the opposite—that private ownership of handguns actually reduces crime rates. This argument received nationwide attention in 1998 with the publication of economist John R. Lott Jr.'s book *More Guns, Less Crime*. In the book, Lott uses detailed statistical analysis of crime data to support the view, long embraced by gun advocates, that criminals are less likely to act against potential victims that may be armed. Florida State University criminologist Gary Kleck sums up the argument this way: "Gun use by private citizens against violent criminals and burglars is a more common negative consequence for violent criminals than legal actions like arrests."

Lott's research has been widely criticized by gun control groups, who point to other statistical analyses to counter Lott's claims. For example, in October 2001 economist Mark Duggan published a study concluding that "increases in gun ownership lead to substantial increases in the overall homicide rate." Moreover, gun control advocates argue that the widespread availability of firearms increases the *lethality* of violent crime. In their book *Crime Is Not the Problem: Lethal Violence in America*, authors Franklin Zimring and Gordon Hawkins conclude that "the ready availability of guns . . . is the most important single contribution to the high U.S. death rate from violence. Our rate of assault is not exceptional; our death rate from assault is exceptional."

One point that both sides of the gun control debate agree on is that gun crime is a serious problem. What should be done about it, however, is a contentious issue that the authors of the following viewpoints address.

"Not surprisingly, the more guns there are, the more gun crime there is."

Gun Control Laws Can Reduce Violent Crime

Garen Wintemute

Garen Wintemute is director of the Violence Prevention Research Program at the University of California, Davis, and the author of *The Crime Drop in America*, from which the following viewpoint is excerpted. In it he discusses the decline in firearm violence that the United States has experienced since 1993 and attributes this decline to the success of several gun control initiatives. For example, he notes, in the 1990s many cities enforced gun laws more strictly and many states increased the sentences for gun crimes. The federal government also reduced the number of licensed firearms dealers. Perhaps most importantly, the federal Brady Act introduced waiting periods in order to reduce criminals' access to guns. While much work remains to be done, concludes Wintemute, these initiatives show that gun control laws can reduce crime.

As you read, consider the following questions:
1. By what percentage did the firearm fatality rate drop from 1993 to 1995, according to Wintemute?
2. How many federally licensed firearms dealers were there in 1993, and how many were there in October 1999, according to the author?
3. What evidence from California does Wintemute cite to support his claim that "screening prospective handgun purchasers does work"?

Garen Wintemute, "Guns and Gun Violence," *The Crime Drop in America*, edited by Alfred Blumstein and Joel Wallman. New York: Cambridge University Press, 2000. Copyright © 2000 by Cambridge University Press. Reproduced by permission.

The United States is experiencing a very rapid decline in rates of serious violence, and particularly firearm violence. As recently as 1993, America's homicide rate was at a near-historic high; by mid-1999 it was lower than at any time since the mid-1960s, and all indications are that it is continuing to fall. This [viewpoint] focuses on some of the most important interventions that have helped reduce gun violence. My discussion is limited to interventions that targeted firearms and firearm violence directly, and mainly to interventions that have been formally evaluated. . . .

The Importance of Guns in Crime and Violence

The United States has experienced a true epidemic of firearm violence. . . . Gun violence accounted for nearly the entire increase, and the more recent decrease, in overall rates of serious violence in the United States. Firearm violence remains very common; as recently as 1998, nearly 700,000 violent crimes were committed with firearms.

There are a great many firearms in the United States. American households contained 192 million firearms in 1994, of which 65 million were handguns. Since 1994, an average of 3.9 million new firearms have been added annually to existing stocks through domestic production alone.

Not surprisingly, the more guns there are, the more gun crime there is. Many correlational studies, some geographic and some temporal, have established a close relationship between gun availability and rates of gun violence at the population level. The equation works for individuals, too; keeping a firearm in the home more than doubles the risk that a member of the household will be killed in a firearm homicide.

Access to firearms facilitates particular types of crimes, such as robbery against "harder" targets. This is particularly the case when the person committing the crime is a stranger to the victim, and such crimes now constitute 44 percent of all violent crimes in the United States.

Firearms modify the consequences of crime. The use of a gun as opposed to some other weapon increases the likelihood that a violent crime will be completed, particularly in the cases of rape and robbery. In 1998, according to police data compiled by the Federal Bureau of Investigation (FBI) in its Uniform Crime Reports (UCR), assaults committed with a firearm were 4.6 times as likely as assaults committed with a knife or similar weapon to result in a fatality. Robberies and family and intimate assaults are three times as likely to result in death when a firearm is involved as when a knife or similar weapon is used. . . .

Explaining the Drop in Gun Crime

In 1998, the Centers for Disease Control and Prevention (CDC) published a detailed study of trends in gun violence in the United States. The rate of both fatal and nonfatal firearm injuries peaked in the third quarter of 1993. By the end of the second quarter of 1995, less than two years after the peak had been reached, there had been a 23 percent decrease in the rate of firearm injuries and a 10 percent drop in the fatality rate. Assaultive injuries among males ages 15 to 24 decreased 28 percent, and fatalities decreased 16.5 percent.

From 1993 to 1998, the number of serious violent crimes in the United States declined substantially. The single greatest percentage decline was seen in firearm robbery. Declines in firearm-related crime were greater than for crimes involving other weapons, so that the percentage of violent crimes that involved firearms also decreased. Among juveniles, homicide arrests decreased 54 percent between 1993 and 1998.

Provisional data for the first half of 1999 suggest that the decline in violent crime has continued; as compared to the first half of 1998, homicide decreased a further 13 percent, robbery 10 percent, and aggravated assault 7 percent. All but homicide decreased in cities of all sizes and in rural areas as well.

Reflecting again the close association between crime rates and gun availability, this downward trend in firearm violence was accompanied by a 58 percent drop in annual production of semiautomatic pistols between 1993 and 1998. The greatest declines were for .25- and .380-caliber guns. . . .

Beginning in the mid-1980s, medical and public health practitioners became increasingly involved in violence prevention. Perhaps their main contribution to the field was their emphasis on the importance of aggregating information on single instances of violence to seek underlying patterns. From cholera outbreaks in London in the eighteenth century to the advent of HIV/AIDS, they had grown used to the precept that such patterns were informative and frequently led to effective prevention measures. Their arrival on the scene coincided with an already increasing interest on the part of criminologists and criminal justice practitioners in applying the lessons learned from such patterns—the "big picture"—at the street level.

In the case of gun violence, the big picture emerged with unexpected clarity. The distribution of gun violence was anything but random. It was highly concentrated in space. Relatively narrow subgroups of the population were at extremely high risk. A subset of weapons was disproportionately involved, and these weapons arrived in the hands of those who misused them by definable pathways. The criminal justice system could be surprisingly tolerant of criminal activity involving guns. Increasingly, interventions were designed with these specific findings in mind.

Focusing on Demand and Use

Changing police practices. In 1994, James Q. Wilson suggested that the best approach to preventing criminals from committing gun crime was to "just take away their guns." The Kansas City Gun Experiment, a controlled experiment that fused science with practical law enforcement, sought to do just that. From July 1992 through January 1993, extra police patrols in a target area focused on gun-crime hot spots that had been identified by crime mapping. The widely publicized patrols were made up of officers working overtime; their mission was "to get guns off the street as cost-effectively as possible." Gun seizures rose by 65 percent to a total of seventy-six, of which twenty-nine were seized by the additional patrols.

Gun crime in the target area decreased by 49 percent during the intervention, but it rose 4 percent in a comparison site where usual police practices were followed. There appeared to be no displacement of crime into neighborhoods surrounding the target area. The gun-crime rate returned toward its pre-intervention level when the intervention ended. It dropped again, although by a smaller amount, when the patrols were reinstituted. . . .

The largest and best known application of gun-oriented policing has been in New York City. Beginning in 1994, the New York Police Department (NYPD) maintained a special Street Crime Unit charged with aggressive enforcement of gun laws. The department targeted gun-crime hot spots and aggressively sought sources of crime guns. From 1994 to 1997, the NYPD made 46,198 gun arrests and confiscated 56,081 firearms. Nonfatal shootings fell by 62 percent from 1993 to 1997. In 1998, New York had just 633 homicides, fewer than in any year since 1964. . . .

Increasing criminal justice sanctions. Federalizing prosecution of some firearm-related crimes has recently received widespread attention. In many cases, federal penalties for possession of firearms by felons and for drug offenses involving the use of firearms are stiffer than those imposed at the state level.

In February 1997, Richmond, Virginia, initiated Project Exile, a practice of screening potential prosecutions and referring to the federal system those in which the potential penalties were tougher there. By February 1999, there had been 404 federal indictments, and the conviction rate was 86 percent. The average prison term was more than 4.5 years. Homicide decreased by 36 percent from 1997 to 1998. Richmond's experience has not been compared to that of cities without such programs, so it is impossible to know for certain that the change in prosecution tactics bears major responsibility for the decrease. . . . Similar programs have since begun in Philadelphia, Rochester, San Francisco–Oakland, and elsewhere. . . .

Focusing on Supply

Limiting the number of dealers. ATF [Bureau of Alcohol, Tobacco, and Firearms] began to tighten oversight of prospective and current dealers in January 1993, under a new National Firearms Program. Inspections were increased, and interviews were required for all new applications and selected renewals. More than 27,000 inspections were conducted in 1993, up from 11,800 in 1990; nearly 18,000 law enforcement referrals were made. These actions were reinforced by the Federal Firearms Licensee Reform Act, adopted in November, which increased licensing fees to $200 for an initial application and $90 for a renewal. New applicants were also required to submit a photograph and fingerprints; background checks were broadened and performed on renewing licensees as well. The 1994 Violent Crime Control and Law Enforcement Act required license holders to certify that they were in compliance with state and local laws and regulations.

Handgun Homicide and Production

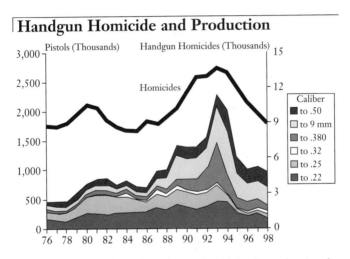

Handgun homicide and semiautomatic pistol production by caliber in the United States from 1976 to 1998. Data from *Homicide Trends in the United States*, Bureau of Justice Statistics, and the Bureau of Alcohol, Tobacco, and Firearms.

Garen Wintemute, "Guns and Gun Violence," in Alfred Blumstein and Joel Wallman, eds., *The Crime Drop in America*. New York: Cambridge University Press, 2000.

The total number of federal firearms license holders (dealers, pawnbrokers, and manufacturers) fell from 287,000 at its peak in 1993 to just 86,180 by October 1999, a 70 percent drop. It is still falling. A 1996 survey by the General Accounting Office found that license holders who were engaged in the legitimate business of selling guns appeared to be relatively unaffected by the changes. Of eighty dealers who had let their licenses expire in late 1994 or early 1995, only two had sold more than 100 guns in an average year.

Other interventions were taken at the state level. . . . North Carolina found in 1993 that only 26 percent of dealers also possessed its required state license. Those in violation included large retail outlets such as Wal-Mart and Kmart. Noncomplying dealers were required either to obtain a state license or to forfeit their federal license. Alabama also identified federal firearms licensees who did not possess its required state license and notified each of them of the requirement. Nine hundred licensed dealers claimed to be ignorant of the requirement, obtained the license, and paid penalties. Another 900 said that they were not actively selling firearms, and 200 more could not be located; licenses for these 1,100 were slated for cancellation. . . .

Perhaps fortunately, in that it will help focus future intervention efforts, a very small fraction of licensed dealers still accounts for a very large share of crime guns, at least as reflected by ATF's tracing data. A recent study focused on nationwide traces for 1996–97. Of 89,771 dealers in all, just 89—0.1 percent of the total—had more than 100 traced guns linked to each and together accounted for 23 percent of all traced guns. Another 415 dealers, each involved in between 25 and 99 gun traces, accounted for another 23 percent of traces.

Given the increasing awareness of the importance of new guns among those used in crime, this study also focused on dealers with traced guns having a short average time from sale to crime-related confiscation, known as "time-to-crime." Just seventy-five dealers with an average time-to-crime of under three years for their traced guns accounted for 20 percent of all traces.

Future enforcement efforts are likely to focus on dealers who sell a disproportionately high number of guns that are later used in crime or who report frequent thefts. The number of dealers will also probably continue to decrease; there are only 15,000 to 20,000 gun stores in the United States, still far fewer than the number of licensed dealers. . . .

Limiting gun sales. Evidence that firearms acquired in multiple-purchase transactions were likely to be trafficked and used in crime led to restrictions on such purchases at the state level. Virginia adopted a law, effective in July 1993, that limited purchases of firearms by persons other than dealers to no more than one per month. Prior to that time, Virginia had been recognized as a major source of crime guns confiscated in other states, particularly in New England, that had more restrictive laws on gun purchase. Virginia was the source of 35 percent of crime guns confiscated in New England that were purchased before the effective date of the law, but just 16 percent of guns purchased later. Maryland followed suit in 1996, and California in 1999.

A national one-gun-a-month policy would prevent the illegal firearms market from shifting to new sources of supply as individual states restrict or eliminate multiple purchases. Such a policy is supported by 81 percent of the general public and 53 percent of gun owners.

Restrictions on buyers. Federal law has long prohibited felons, persons under felony indictment, controlled-substance users, and certain others from possessing firearms. The Gun Control Act of 1968 required prospective purchasers to certify that they were not a member of one of the prohibited classes, but did not require a background check to verify that these certifications were valid. A number of states instituted background checks on their own, and found that 1 to 2 percent of prospective handgun purchasers were prohibited persons.

The Brady Act

Federal requirements changed in 1994 following the enactment of the Brady Handgun Violence Prevention Act. The Brady Act required a five-day waiting period prior to handgun purchase, and initially also required a designated state or local chief law enforcement officer to conduct a criminal records background check. The latter requirement was declared unconstitutional by the Supreme Court in June 1997. Most chief law enforcement officers continued to perform background checks on a voluntary basis.

By 1998, twenty-three states operated under the provisions of the Brady Act. The others, known as "Brady alternative" states, had screening requirements that were at least as restrictive as Brady and operated under their state statutes. Over the five years that Brady had been in operation, all states together had screened a total of 12.7 million applications to purchase guns and had issued 312,000 denials, including 207,000 for prior felony convictions or pending indictments.

Procedures for screening handgun purchasers in the Brady states were reconfigured in November 1998. The waiting period and the background checks conducted by state or local law enforcement agencies were replaced by a National Instant Check System (NICS) administered by the FBI. During NICS's first year of operation, nearly 90 percent of background checks were completed within two hours of application; 72 percent were completed within thirty seconds. Difficult checks could take several days, however, and the law allowed dealers to release firearms to purchasers after three business days, whether or not the background checks were completed. By the end of 1999, 3,353 prohibited persons, most of them felons, had acquired firearms in this manner; just 442 had surrendered their guns. This problem would largely be eliminated if the waiting period for firearm purchases were lengthened.

Critics of programs to screen prospective purchasers of firearms suggested that they were unlikely to be effective. They argued that those with criminal intent who were prevented from buying firearms in the legal market would simply acquire them illegally. The provisions of the Brady Act were described as a "sop to the widespread fear of crime." But screening prospective handgun purchasers does work. It reduces risk for later criminal activity among felons whose applications to purchase handguns are denied. In a recent California study, 170 felons whose handgun purchases were denied were compared to 2,470 handgun buyers who had felony arrests but no felony convictions. Over three years of follow-up, the felony arrestees whose purchases were approved were 21 percent more likely to be charged with a new gun offense, and 24 percent more likely to be charged with a new violent offense, than the convicted felons were. In Florida, a significant decrease in homicide rates followed that state's adoption of a mandatory waiting period and background check for handgun purchase.

Critics on the other side of the issue suggested that denying the purchase or possession of a firearm based on a prior felony conviction or indictment did not go far enough. The 1997 Omnibus Consolidated Appropriations Act banned the purchase or possession of firearms by persons convicted of a misdemeanor domestic-violence offense. Persons subject to active domestic-violence restraining orders had been prohibited from purchasing or possessing handguns since 1994. . . .

As with felons, making it more difficult for misdemeanants to acquire handguns appears to be effective. A California study of violent misdemeanants who sought to purchase handguns found that denying handgun purchase appeared to reduce their risk of committing new crimes involving guns or violence by 20 to 30 percent. A majority of firearms owners, let alone members of the general public, supports denying firearms purchases to persons who had been convicted of misdemeanors involving firearms, violence, or substance abuse. . . .

Banning Handguns

Several major cities largely banned the purchase or possession of handguns, exempting those that were legally owned at the time the legislation became effective. The effectiveness of local bans is partly undermined by widespread trafficking in firearms: if guns are hard to purchase legally in a particular jurisdiction, they can simply be brought in from elsewhere. However, the new and more effective measures to disrupt gun trafficking may make local bans a more attractive option in the future.

In 1976, Washington, DC, banned the purchase and sale of handguns and the possession of all handguns that were not previously owned and registered. Violations of the law were misdemeanors. Passage of the law was followed by a 25 percent drop in firearm homicide. There was no parallel decrease in homicide using other weapons, which would have suggested that the decrease in gun homicides was related to some external factor. Nor was there an increase in homicide by other means, suggesting that the law did not simply cause other weapons to be substituted for firearms. In addition, there was no change in either firearm or nonfirearm homicide in nearby areas of Maryland or Virginia. The effect persisted through 1987. Soon thereafter, as crack cocaine became common in the District, the effects of the law were overwhelmed by drug-related shootings.

New York City's Sullivan Law has largely banned the purchase of handguns since 1911. A controlled evaluation of the law has never been conducted, but for much of the twentieth century the city's homicide rate was substantially lower than that for the country's other largest cities. One of the major effects of the law was to alter the dynamics of the illegal firearms market. Nearly 85 percent of crime guns recovered by New York City law enforcement agencies are imported from outside the state. . . .

Building on Success

In the near future, many of these successful interventions will become more widespread. . . . Focused law enforcement and increased sanctions will raise the cost of doing gun crime. Other interventions will decrease the supply of firearms for criminal use. Firearms trafficking will become more difficult and dangerous. Dealers who furnish guns for crime will be the target of more aggressive identification and prosecution efforts. Manufacturers now face the real possibility that they will be held accountable in court for crimes arising in part from their manufacturing and distribution practices. In March 2000, precisely to avoid such liability, Smith & Wesson, the country's largest handgun manufacturer, agreed to incorporate an array of safety features into its products and restructure its distribution procedures.

Much work remains to be done, and progress will not go uninterrupted. In 1999 a trend toward increasing homicide rates developed in the nation's largest cities: one percent overall and 9 percent in New York City. Nonetheless, while it would be foolish to make firm predictions, there is good reason to expect that overall rates of gun violence will continue to decrease.

"Why would gun controls be any more effective in keeping guns out of the criminal subculture than drug controls in keeping illicit drugs out of the drug subculture?"

Most Gun Control Laws Are Ineffective

James B. Jacobs

James B. Jacobs is a professor of law at New York University and the author of *Can Gun Control Work?*, from which the following viewpoint is excerpted. In it he argues that most gun control initiatives in the United States are misguided because they seek to keep guns out of the hands of citizens and criminals alike. Jacobs writes that efforts to reduce access to guns—such as background checks for gun purchasers or bans on assault weapons or handguns—are futile, since criminals can easily obtain guns through the black market. Instead of gun prohibition, Jacobs argues that gun control initiatives should focus on cracking down on gun crimes and encouraging responsible gun ownership and use among civilians.

As you read, consider the following questions:
1. What are the four kinds of gun crime that Jacobs describes?
2. According to Jacobs, the top priority for the United States in the area of gun violence should be to enforce what message?
3. What are some of the ways that criminals circumvent the Brady Law, in the author's view?

Gun "control" should be about reinforcing a norm of responsible gun ownership and use. We should approach the use of guns with the same mindset that we approach alcohol consumption and driving. These are dangerous activities that must be approached with maturity and caution. We talk about "responsible drinking" and "safe driving," not about drinking and driving controls. Firearms accidents are clearly a gun problem just as automobile accidents are a car problem. It ought to be cause for optimism that accidental firearms deaths have been decreasing for decades, despite a steady increase in the number of firearms. If there were no firearms, no swimming pools, and no automobiles, the number of accidental deaths would greatly decrease. But eliminating swimming pools, cars, or guns are not realistic options. . . .

Criminals Will Circumvent Gun Control Laws

Gun crime is by far our most serious firearms problem. However, gun crime itself is not a single phenomenon or homogeneous category. Breaking gun crime down into several broad categories helps us to think about (1) the extent to which the availability of guns causes crime, and (2) the potential and limits of various gun controls. First, there is gun crime committed by career offenders, including professional bank robbers, members of Cosa Nostra [Mafia], drug cartels, drug distribution networks, and street gangs. It is simplistic to label guns the *cause* of this kind of criminality, although guns certainly make such groups more dangerous. There is no possibility that any gun control policy could succeed in denying the members of these groups access to firearms. Indeed, even in Japan, where there is very little private ownership of guns, members of the Yakuza and other organized crime groups have no difficulty obtaining firearms. In the United States, career criminals possess, carry, and use guns, despite the threat of draconian punishment under state and federal felon-in-possession laws and of sentence enhancements for committing crimes with a gun.

Second, there is "disorganized" gun crime, like carjacking and armed robbery of stores, gas stations, and pedestrians, carried out by individuals alone or in twos or threes. This is the kind of street crime that terrifies the public. The people who commit such crimes are often young, poor, and heavily involved with drugs. They may kill people in botched robberies or for no apparent reason. They often kill one another. Their stray bullets may kill or injure bystanders. From their own experiences in juvenile detention centers, reformatories, adult jails and prisons, and in the criminal subculture, individuals in this category have many sources—family members, friends, gang associates, drug dealers, and professional fences—from whom they can purchase or borrow handguns. It seems highly unlikely that any gun control regime could prevent such individuals from obtaining firearms. They rarely purchase guns from FFLs [Federal Firearm License Holders], so more stringent regulation of licensed retail sellers would have little, if any, impact. Why would gun controls be any more effective in keeping guns out of the criminal subculture than drug controls in keeping illicit drugs out of the drug subculture?

Professors [Philip] Cook and [Jens] Ludwig suggest, almost in passing, that if the price of firearms increased (via enforcement and regulatory strategies or by taxation), some poor young offenders would not have the money or choose not to spend their money on a gun. I have no objection to increasing the tax on handguns, if for no other purpose than to fund victims' services, but I fear that the demand for firearms will prove far more inelastic than Cook and Ludwig imagine. Young men, albeit poor, living in tough neighborhoods will come up with an additional $10, $20, or $30 to purchase a firearm if they perceive that it is essential to their survival, status, or criminal opportunities. Indeed, several researchers, including, most recently, Anthony Braga and his colleagues in Boston, have found that street criminals do not prefer cheap guns. According to Braga et al., gang members in Boston prefer relatively expensive high caliber handguns rather than the cheapest guns. Guns are not expensive, cost no more than a fancy pair of sneakers, and far less than even casual use of drugs. In any event, an impecunious youth living in a tough neighborhood can likely share or borrow a gun. This kind of criminality must be addressed by targeting gun criminals with vigorous policing, prosecution, and long incarcerative sentences, and by effective social welfare programs and employment and education initiatives. "Supply side" gun strategies hold very little promise.

The Extent of Spontaneous Gun Violence Is Exaggerated

Third, there are gun crimes committed by friends, spouses, and lovers against one another. It is here that gun controls have the most promise. Undoubtedly, there are shootings which are predominantly situational; without the presence of a gun, such incidents would not occur or they would result in less injury. But the frequency of spontaneous lethal violence by essentially law-abiding individuals is frequently exaggerated. The great majority of people who kill their "acquaintances" have substantial criminal records. Most of the victims also have criminal records. Some victims coded as "acquaintances" are actually members of rival gangs or drug networks or are rivals within the same group. A high percentage of the "relationships" that spawn lethal violence have been marred by a long history of conflict and violence. The reality of such killings is hardly captured by the term "situational."

Even killings of intimate partners are rarely the product of a mere lover's quarrel or a jealous rage. Most serious and lethal domestic violence is not the result of an argument that got out of hand between an otherwise harmonious couple. Far more frequently, a domestic violence killing is the culmination of months or years of abuse and beatings, that is, the product of a relationship spiraling ever downward. (One thinks of Nicole Brown Simpson, predicting that her ex-husband would someday kill her.) These are not the kind of situations where absence of a gun means that the conflict will blow over and the marriage return to happy homeostasis. (Nicole Brown Simpson, of course, was stabbed to death.) It would be a mistake to assume that killings between intimates are usually the result of spur-of-the-moment explosions of violence. Some defendants have planned their murderous conduct over a substantial period of time. They may have coolly decided that their spouse or business partner is worth more dead than alive. They may have stalked a former lover for months. They may have harbored a murderous plan for years. Even a momentary murderous rage can be so powerful that the aggressor will not stop short of killing the victim, with or without a gun. People who live in the same household have many opportunities and many weapons to kill one another—for example, with knives, bottles, cords, bats, poisons, or even bare hands.

Of course, men with domestic violence convictions or restraining orders *ought to be prevented* from purchasing and possessing firearms, at least while their relationship with the victim continues to simmer. But this is easier said than done in contemporary American society, where there are so many routes to obtaining a gun. It would not be wise to put much faith in the efficacy of a gun control scheme to protect the vulnerable partner. It makes more sense to invest in safe houses for the victims of domestic violence.

Background Checks and Waiting Periods

Is there any way to prevent people without a criminal record from obtaining guns? A Brady background check will not exclude people who do not have a prior criminal record from making purchases in the primary market, much less at gun shows and in the secondary market generally. . . . It would be a tremendous, probably insoluble, logistical and enforcement challenge to regulate secondary firearms sales. And even if that were somehow accomplished, the market in stolen and trafficked guns would remain.

A waiting period could prevent a person in a murderous rage from running out of the house, job site, or bar and, on the spot, purchasing a firearm from an FFL, then rushing back home to use it on his spouse or lover. A waiting period imposes a time period of several days or longer during which tempers can cool, so that by the time the gun is obtained, the motivation to kill will have evaporated. Perhaps a waiting period also makes an important symbolic statement: a gun purchase is a serious matter and it should be undertaken soberly, more slowly, and more deliberately than the ordinary consumer purchase.

My guess is that cases in which an enraged killer runs to a store, buys a gun, and immediately shoots his victim are *extremely rare* (I have never seen any data on the frequency of such events), but the cost of implementing a waiting period is very low. Interim Brady established a de facto waiting period of five (business) days. Permanent Brady allows NICS [National Instant Criminal Background Check System] up to three days to approve a sale, but most sales are approved immediately. A person without a disqualifying record can walk into a gun store and leave with a gun in under an hour.

Most Violent Crimes Do Not Involve Guns

Violent Crimes Committed with a Firearm, 1999

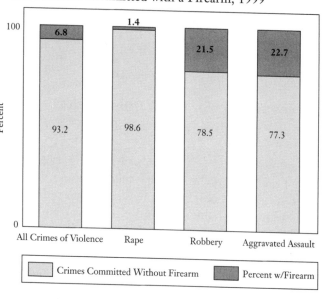

James B. Jacobs, *Can Gun Control Work?* New York: Oxford University Press, 2002.

Many states (like California and Florida) have additional waiting periods. But waiting periods do not apply to gun purchases from nondealers. The enraged individual could instantly borrow a gun from a friend or colleague or from someone advertising in the local paper. Of course, a waiting period would have no effect on an enraged individual who already owns a gun or who can lethally deploy a knife, baseball bat, or some other weapon. Moreover, the NRA [National Rifle Association] has a point in noting that, in some cases, a waiting period could deny a firearm to a person under immediate threat who has no other viable means of self-defense. Thus, a waiting period ought to be linked to a law enforcement commitment to protect the individual facing a serious threat.

A fourth category of gun crime involves rampages, such as what happened at Columbine High School and at the Jewish Community Center in Granada Hills, California. The enormity of these tragedies understandably provokes calls *to do something*. But what? Those who commit such atrocities usually develop their plans over many months and may be indifferent to or even hoping for their own death. Thus, they can take whatever time is necessary to obtain a firearm from a dealer or nondealer, or they can steal a gun. The two students who carried out the indiscriminate murder of classmates at Columbine High School planned to and did kill themselves after shooting as many of their schoolmates as possible. It is difficult to imagine any regulatory regime that could have prevented them from obtaining the firearms necessary to achieve that goal. Probably the only way, if there is a way, to prevent such tragedies is obtaining and acting on information about students or others who are behaving curiously, talking about revenge killings, or otherwise signaling an impending rampage. Sadly, we probably also need armed security personnel and perhaps a few armed teachers able to respond effectively in the event that a rampage occurs. . . .

Tough Treatment for Gun Offenders

By far, the easiest firearms policy for the United States is to provide severe punishment for every defendant who uses a firearm in the commission of a crime. There are no interest groups that oppose tough treatment for gun offenders. Indeed, the NRA, the police, and victims groups all support long prison terms for individuals who commit crimes with guns. We should retrace a line that has been drawn in the sand for a long time: gun crime will be severely punished. Enforcing that message vigorously and consistently in federal and state court should be our top priority in the area of gun violence. Specialized prosecution units and even specialized gun courts (that only deal with defendants charged with gun crimes) would help to assure that no armed offender falls between the cracks. Offenders who use guns should not get probation and not qualify for early release from prison. . . .

Preventing Access to Firearms: A Dose of Realism

The most unrealistic control policy for the United States is prohibition of private ownership of firearms or just handguns. Demanding disarmament, as the Communitarian Network, the Surgeon General's Task Force, and others have done, serves no useful purpose and only fans the flames of a culture war between gun owners and gun controllers, who in fighting with one another forget that the violent crime problem is the source of our concern.

Furthermore, talk of disarmament is counterproductive; it reinforces the resolve of gun owners to resist all gun controls because they are steps down a path to involuntary disarmament. Any serious effort to pass a firearms disarmament plan would trigger massive gun acquisition and expand and radicalize a resistance movement. The last thing the U.S. government needs is endless conflict with a huge segment of the citizenry that has never committed a gun crime. A war on civilian gun ownership would undermine crime prevention by unnecessarily diverting resources from preventing and solving crime. . . .

The dominant American twentieth-century firearms policy of trying to keep guns out of the hands of dangerous individuals by regulating federally licensed dealers has reached a dead end. It would be very difficult to elaborate this strategy beyond the Brady Law. And the Brady Law itself, passed to give teeth to the Federal Firearms Act and Gun Control Act, can be easily circumvented by ineligible purchasers. They need only find a straw purchaser willing to buy a gun for them, or buy a gun themselves at a gun show or from a nondealer who is selling a gun through a newspaper ad or by word of mouth. Closing the gun show loophole, by extending Brady to all gun show sales, would be another weak measure, if all other secondary sales by nondealers remain unregulated. . . .

Cause for Optimism

All this might leave some readers with a feeling of despair. But there is more reason for optimism now then there was one or two decades ago. Violence has decreased dramatically in the last decade in the United States, despite the continued increase in the stock of civilian guns. This means that firearms accessibility is not the only thing, and not the most important thing, driving gun crime. Criminologists and policy makers should not be distracted by unrealistic proposals and slogans for "gun control." Rather, they should look to building on other anti-crime strategies and constructive social welfare policies that might be contributing to this unprecedented decrease of violent crime and gun crime.

"*Guns do make it easier to commit bad deeds, but they also make it easier for people to defend themselves where few alternatives are available.*"

Gun Ownership Reduces Crime

John R. Lott Jr.

John R. Lott Jr. is a resident scholar at the American Enterprise Institute, as well as the author of *More Guns, Less Crime* and *The Bias Against Guns*, from which the following viewpoint is adapted. Lott maintains that guns are used to defend against crimes more often than they are to commit them. However, he notes, examples of defensive gun use are deliberately downplayed by the mainstream media. Lott cites specific examples of defensive gun use as well as an incident in which mainstream newspapers did not report on how defensive gun use ended a high-profile school shooting. The author contends that the pervasive pro–gun control bias in newspaper, radio, and TV reporting has caused most Americans to erroneously believe that gun ownership contributes to crime.

As you read, consider the following questions:
1. How many instances of defensive gun use occurred nationwide in 2001, according to the author?
2. In Lott's view, what is the safest way to respond to any type of criminal assault?
3. In Lott's opinion, what assumption is implicit in most polls on gun control?

I often give talks to audiences explaining that research by me and others shows that guns are used much more often to fend off crimes than to commit them. People are very surprised to learn that survey data show that guns are used defensively by private citizens in the U.S. anywhere from 1.5 to 3.4 million times a year. A question I hear repeatedly is: "If defensive gun use occurs so often, why haven't I ever heard of even one story?"

Defensive Gun Use Is Widespread

Obviously anecdotal stories published in newspapers can't prove how numerous these events are, but they can at least deal with the question of whether these events even occur. During 2001, I did two detailed searches on defensive gun uses: one for the period covering March 11 to 17 of that year, and another for the period July 22 to 28. While these searches were not meant to be comprehensive, I found a total of 40 defensive gun uses over those two weeks. Some representative examples:

Clearwater, Florida: At 1:05 A.M., a man started banging on a patio door, beat on a family's truck, then tore open the patio door. After numerous shouted warnings not to break into the home, a 16-year-old boy fired a single rifle shot, wounding the attacker.

Columbia, South Carolina: As two gas station employees left work just after midnight, two men attempted to rob them, beating them about the head and neck with a shovel handle. The male employee broke away long enough to draw a handgun from his pocket and shot at his attacker, who later died.

Detroit, Michigan: A mentally disturbed man wailed that the President was going to have him killed, and started firing at people in passing cars. A man at the scene who had a permit to carry a concealed handgun fired shots that forced the attacker to run away.

West Palm Beach, Florida: After being beaten during a robbery at his home, a homeowner began carrying a handgun in his pocket. When another robber attacked him just two days later the homeowner shot and wounded his assailant.

Columbia Falls, Montana: A woman's ex-boyfriend entered her home to sexually assault her. She got away long enough to get her pistol and hold her attacker at gun point until police arrived.

Baton Rouge, Louisiana: At 5:45 A.M., a crack addict kicked in the back door of a house and charged the home-owner, who shot him to death.

Gainesville, Florida: A newspaper carrier was dragged from his car and beaten by five men at 3:15 A.M. The victim then shot one of the attackers in the chest with a concealed weapon.

Tampa, Florida: Two teenage armed robbers went on a four-hour crime spree, hijacking cars, robbing people, and hospitalizing one victim with serious injuries. They were stopped when one intended victim, a pizza-store owner, shot and wounded one attacker.

Charleston, South Carolina: A carjacking was stopped by a 27-year-old victim who then shot one of his attackers. The victim had paused to ask directions when several men, one with a lengthy criminal record, jumped into the car.

These life and death stories represent only a tiny fraction of defensive gun uses. A survey of 1,015 people I conducted during November and December 2002 indicates that 2.3 million defensive gun uses occurred nationwide in 2001. Guns do make it easier to commit bad deeds, but they also make it easier for people to defend themselves where few alternatives are available. That is why it is so important that people receive an accurate, balanced accounting of how guns are used. Unfortunately, the media are doing a very poor job of that today.

Defensive Gun Use Is Underreported

Though my survey indicates that simply brandishing a gun stops crimes 95 percent of the time, it is very rare to see a story of such an event reported in the media. A dead gunshot victim on the ground is highly newsworthy, while a criminal fleeing after a woman points a gun is apparently not considered news at all. That's not impossible to understand; after all, no shots were fired, no crime was committed, and no one is even sure what crime would have been committed had a weapon not been drawn.

In other words, airplane crashes get news coverage, while successful take-offs and landings do not. Even though fewer than one out of 1,000 defensive gun uses result in the death of the attacker, the newsman's penchant for drama means that the bloodier cases are usually covered. Even in the rare cases where guns are used to shoot someone, injuries are about six times more frequent than deaths. You wouldn't know this from the stories the media choose to report.

But much more than a bias toward bad news and drama goes into the media's selective reporting on gun usage. Why, for instance, does the torrential coverage of public shooting sprees fail to acknowledge when such attacks are aborted by citizens with guns? In January 2002, a shooting left three dead at the Appalachian Law School in Virginia. The event made international headlines and produced more calls for gun control.

Yet one critical fact was missing from virtually all the news coverage: The attack was stopped by two students who had guns in their cars.

The fast responses of Mikael Gross and Tracy Bridges undoubtedly saved many lives. Mikael was outside the law school returning from lunch when Peter Odighizuwa started shooting. Tracy was in a classroom waiting for class to start. When the shots rang out, chaos erupted. Mikael and Tracy were prepared to do something more constructive: Both immediately ran to their cars and got their guns, then approached the shooter from different sides. Thus confronted, the attacker threw his gun down.

Isn't it remarkable that out of 208 news stories (from a Lexis-Nexis search) in the week after the event, just four mentioned that the students who stopped the shooter had guns? A typical description of the event in the *Washington Post*. "Three students pounced on the gunman and held him until help arrived." New York's *Newsday* noted only that the attacker was "restrained by students." Many stories mentioned the law-enforcement or military backgrounds of these student heroes, but virtually all of the media, in discussing how the killer was stopped, said things such as: "students tackled the man while he was still armed" "students tackled the gunman" the attacker "dropped his gun after being confronted by students, who then tackled him to the ground" or "students ended the rampage by confronting and then tackling the gunman, who dropped his weapon."

In all, 72 stories described how the attacker was stopped, without mentioning that the heroes had guns. Yet 68 stories provided precise details on the gun used by the attacker: The *New York Times* made sure to point out it was "a .380 semi-automatic handgun"; the *Los Angeles Times* noted it was "a .380-caliber semiautomatic pistol."

A week and a half after the assault, I appeared on a radio program in Los Angeles along with Tracy Bridges, one of the Appalachian Law School heroes. Tracy related how "shocked" he had been by the news coverage. Though he had carefully described to over 50 reporters what had happened, explaining how he had to point his gun at the attacker and yell at him to drop his gun, the media had consistently reported that the incident had ended by the students "tackling" the killer. When I relayed what the *Washington Post* had reported, Tracy quickly mentioned that he had spent a considerable amount of time talking face-to-face with reporter Maria Glod of the *Post*. He seemed stunned that this conversation had not resulted in a more accurate rendition of what had occurred. . . .

Systematic Suppression of Information on How Guns Deter Crime

Selective reporting of crimes such as the Appalachian Law School incident isn't just poor journalism; it could actually endanger people's lives. By turning a case of defensive gun use into a situation where students merely "overpowered a gunman" the media give potential victims the wrong impression of what works when confronted with violence. Research consistently shows that having a gun (usually just showing it) is the safest way to respond to any type of criminal assault.

It's no wonder people find it hard to believe that guns are used in self-defense 2 million times a year: Reporting on these events is systematically suppressed. When was the last time you saw a story in the national news about a private citizen using his gun to stop a crime? Media decisions to cover only the crimes committed with guns—and not the crimes stopped with them—have a real impact on people's perceptions of the desirability of guns.

To flesh out this impression with some data, I conducted searches of the nation's three largest newspapers—*USA Today*, the *Wall Street Journal*, and the *New York Times*—for the year 2001 and found that only the *Times* carried even a single news story on defensive gun use. (The instance involved a retired New York City Department of Corrections worker who shot a man who was holding up a gas station.) Broadening my search to the top ten newspapers in the country, I learned that the *Los Angeles Times*, *Washington Post*, and *Chicago Tribune* each managed to report three such stories in a year.

Asay. © 1999 by the Creators Syndicate, Inc. Reproduced by permission.

To gain further perspective, I did deeper searches comparing the number of words newspapers published on the use of guns for committing crimes versus stopping crimes. For 2001, I found that the *New York Times* published 104 gun-crime news articles—ranging from a short blurb about a bar fight to a front-page story on a school shooting—for a total of 50,745 words. In comparison, its single story about a gun used in self-defense amounted to all of 163 words. *USA Today* contained 5,660 words on crimes committed with guns, and not a single word on defensive gun use. The least lopsided coverage was provided by the *Washington Post*, with 46,884 words on crimes committed with guns and 953 words on defensive stories—still not exactly a balanced treatment.

Moreover, the few defensive news stories that got coverage were almost all local stories. Though articles about gun crimes are treated as both local and national stories, defensive uses of guns are given only local coverage in the rare instances they run at all. In the full sample of defensive gun-use stories I have collected, less than 1 percent ran outside the local coverage area. News about guns only seems to travel if it's bad.

This helps explain why residents of urban areas are so in favor of gun control. Most crime occurs in the biggest cities, and urbanites are bombarded with tales of gun-facilitated crime. It happens that most defensive gun uses also occur in these same big cities, but they simply aren't reported.

This imbalance isn't just limited to newspapers. Take the 1999 special issue of *Newsweek* entitled "America Under the Gun." Though over 15,000 words and numerous graphics were provided on the topic of gun ownership, there was not one mention of self-defense with a firearm. Under the heading "America's Weapons of Choice," the table captions were: "Top firearms traced to crimes, 1998"; "Firearm deaths per 100,000 people"; and "Percent of homicides using firearms." Nothing at all on "Top firearms used in self-defense," or "Rapes, homicides, and other crimes averted with firearms." The magazine's graphic, gut-wrenching pictures all showed people who had been wounded by guns. No images were offered of people who had used guns to save lives or prevent injuries.

To investigate television coverage, I collected stories reported during 2001 on the evening news broadcasts and morning news shows of ABC, CBS, and NBC. Several segments focused on the increase in gun sales after September 11, and a few of these shows actually went so far as to list the desire for self-defense as a reason for that increase. But despite slightly over 190,000 words of coverage on gun crimes, merely 580 words, on a single news broadcast, were devoted to the use of a gun to block crime—a story about an off-duty police officer who helped stop a school shooting. Not one of the networks mentioned any other defensive gun use—certainly not one carried out by a civilian.

Bias in Source Quotes and Polling Questions

Another place where the predilections of reporters color the news about guns is in the choice of authorities quoted. An analysis of *New York Times* news articles over the last two years reveals that *Times* reporters overwhelmingly cite pro-gun-control academics in their articles. From February 2000 to February 2002, the *Times* cited nine strongly pro-control academics a total of 20 times; one neutral academic once; and no academic who was skeptical that gun control reduces crime. Not once. The same pro-control academics were referenced again and again: Philip Cook of Duke, Alfred Blumstein at Carnegie Mellon, Garen Wintemute of the University of California at Davis.

This imbalance in experts interviewed cannot be explained away by an inability to find academics who are dubious about most gun control laws. Two hundred ninety-four academics from institutions as diverse as Harvard, Stanford, Northwestern, the University of Pennsylvania, and UCLA released an open letter to Congress in 1999 stating that the new gun laws, being proposed at that time were "ill advised." These professors were economists, lawyers, and criminologists. None of these academics was quoted in *New York Times* reports on guns over a two-year period.

Polls frequently serve as the basis of news stories. While they can provide us with important insights about people's views, polls can also mislead in subtle ways. In the case of weapons, poll questions are almost always phrased with the assumption that gun control is either a good thing or, at worst, merely ineffective. The possibility that it could have bad results and even increase crime is never acknowledged. Consider these questions from some well-known national polls:

- Do you think that stricter gun control laws would reduce the amount of violent crime in this country a lot, a little, or not at all? (Pew Research Center/*Newsweek*)

- Do you think stricter gun control laws would reduce the amount of violent crime in this country, or not? (ABC News/*Washington Post*)
- Do you think stricter gun control laws would, or would not reduce violent crime? (CBS News)

I reviewed 17 national and seven state surveys and found that all asked only whether gun control laws reduce crime; not one offered respondents a chance to consider whether gun control might increase crime. This notion apparently never entered the pollsters' minds. . . .

When the possibility that gun control could cause crime is removed from polls, this affects the terms of national debate. When people who hold this view never even hear their opinions mentioned in polls and news stories, they begin to think no one else shares their view. Repeated surveys that imply gun control either makes society better or has no impact gradually acculturate Americans to accepting the view that is constantly presented. . . .

Exaggerating the Risks of Accidental Gun Violence

A final area strongly affected by the media's anti-gun bias is that of accidental shootings. When it comes to this, reporters are eager to write about guns. Many have seen the public service ads showing the voices or pictures of children between the ages of four and eight, implying that there is an epidemic of accidental deaths of these young children.

Data I have collected show that accidental shooters overwhelmingly are adults with long histories of arrests for violent crimes, alcoholism, suspended or revoked drivers licenses, and involvement in car crashes. Meanwhile, the annual number of accidental gun deaths involving children under ten—most of these being cases where someone older shoots the child—is consistently a single digit number. It is a kind of media archetype story, to report on "naturally curious" children shooting themselves or other children—though from 1995 to 1999 the entire United States saw only between five and nine cases a year where a child under ten either accidentally shot themselves or another child.

The danger of children stumbling across guns pales in comparison to many other risks. Over 1,260 children under ten died in cars in 1999. Another 370 died as pedestrians hit by cars. Accidents involving residential fires took 484 children's lives. Bicycles are much more likely to result in accidental deaths than guns. Fully 93 children under the age of ten drowned accidentally in bathtubs. Thirty-six children under five drowned in buckets during 1998. In fact, the number of children under ten who die from any type of accidental gunshot is smaller than the number of toddlers who drown in buckets. Yet few reporters crusade against buckets or bathtubs.

When crimes are committed with guns, there is a somewhat natural inclination toward eliminating all guns. While understandable, this reaction actually endangers people's lives because it ignores how important guns are in protecting people from harm. Unbalanced media coverage exaggerates this, leaving most Americans with a glaringly incomplete picture of the dangers and benefits of firearms. This is how the media bias against guns hurts society, and costs lives.

"Guns are used in 65% of homicides and 59% of all suicides. . . . It is simply too easy in today's society to pull the trigger to end a temporary episode of depression or rage."

Gun Ownership Increases Crime

Steven Riczo

Steven Riczo is director of ambulatory operations at the University Hospitals Health System in Beachwood, Ohio. In the following viewpoint he maintains that the United States has the highest gun homicide rate of any developed nation because Americans have the highest gun ownership rate of any developed nation. Riczo argues that guns are used in homicides, suicides, and unintentional shootings much more often than they are used in self-defense, and he concludes that gun ownership is a major factor behind violent crime. To reduce gun crime and violence, he writes, Americans must embrace rational gun control policies, such as licensing of gun owners and registration of firearms.

As you read, consider the following questions:

1. Approximately how many guns does the author say that Americans own?
2. According to FBI data, what percentage of violent-crime victims use a firearm to defend themselves?
3. According to the author, for every time that a citizen uses a firearm in a justifiable homicide, how many people die as a result of murder, suicide, or unintentional shooting using a gun?

Steven Riczo, "Guns, America, and the 21st Century," *USA Today*, vol. 129, March 2001, p. 16. Copyright © 2001 by the Society for the Advancement of Education. Reproduced by permission.

As Americans become sickened by one firearm tragedy after another, the momentum may be building for a shift in the nation's approach to guns in the 21st century. While it is certainly true that the U.S. has had a tradition of gun ownership, much has changed since the days of the Wild West. This is the age of the Internet, instant global communications, medical marvels, genetic engineering, and other technological wonders that are transforming our lives. Citizens don't have to give up their fight to own firearms in order to make progress on this issue, but should approach it in a more intelligent manner than the bumper sticker mentality and oversimplistic slogans that have characterized this polarized debate. The real question we should be asking ourselves isn't whether or not the government should curtail the right to own firearms, but, as an American, do I really want to own one? Ownership rights can be balanced with reasonable limits in the quest for a sensible gun policy. . . .

The Cost of Widespread Gun Ownership

Other developed nations are willing to accept a reasonable compromise between ownership rights and common-sense restrictions and tend to view gun policy as part of an overall public health plan. The typical reaction of other developed nations to our frequent firearm tragedies is "only in America." The U.S. has the highest per capita gun ownership among all developed nations. The firearm violence comparisons between the U.S. and other industrialized countries are staggering. According to the Centers for Disease Control, the U.S., one of the richest nations on Earth, suffers "the highest firearm mortality rate." Americans murder each other with guns at a rate 19 times higher than any of the 25 richest nations surveyed by CDC. Since 1960, more than 1,000,000 Americans have died from firearm homicides, suicides, and accidental shootings. Moreover, for every firearm death, there are six nonfatal injuries.

Americans own 200,000,000 guns, of which approximately 70,000,000 are handguns. One interesting feature of the high level of gun ownership is that it is not evenly distributed among its citizens. In the most extensive firearm survey ever conducted in the U.S., the National Institute of

Justice found that 35% of households had guns present. Conversely, this also means that 65% of adults and heads of households have rejected gun ownership.

When asked why they chose not to own a gun, the most common reasons identified were that such weapons are dangerous, "immoral" or otherwise objectionable. Of those who own guns, 46% said they do so for prevention of crime, while the majority cited recreational purposes such as hunting and target shooting. Gun owners predominantly identified the reason for the purchase of rifles as recreation and buying handguns for protection against crime. There is also a stark contrast between gun ownership by region of the country—in descending order, the South, West, Midwest, and Northeast. In Texas, for example, there are 68,000,000 guns, which equates to four for every man, woman, and child.

Americans who currently own guns or are contemplating purchasing one would be well-served by objectively evaluating data from reliable organizations such as the Federal Bureau of Investigation and the Justice Department's Bureau of Justice Statistics. Both have extensive data, including detailed interview information from victims of crime. Simply put, guns are designed to kill, and when you bring one into your home, you increase the risk to yourself and family members. According to the *New England Journal of Medicine*, guns kept in the home for self-protection are 22 times more likely to kill someone you know than to kill in self-defense. According to Physicians for Social Responsibility, when a gun is kept in the home, it is about three times as likely that a death will occur in that household.

The Self-Protection Argument

How are Americans to reconcile the risks to themselves and family members of bringing a gun into the home vs. the odds that they will use the firearm to protect their own lives or property against an intruder? A review of the facts should provide some clarity on which to base a decision. First, interviews with detectives in various police departments revealed that about 90% of residential burglaries occur when the owner or family is not at home. The odds of an American being killed during a burglary is quite low, with 61 such deaths out of 14,088 homicides in 1998.

One also must consider the increased risk to the homeowner in pulling a gun on a felon who could have more firearm experience than the victim. As one Bureau of Alcohol, Tobacco, and Firearms agent described in an interview, a law-abiding citizen pulling a gun for the first time to shoot a criminal is in a very difficult situation. He or she has now forced the hand of the perpetrator in a life-threatening and probably terrifying situation for the homeowner. Unless the homeowner has extensive and regular training in the use of firearms comparable to that received by law enforcement officers or the military, the odds of success are slim.

There were just 195 justifiable homicides in 1998 by private citizens out of more than 12,000,000 reported crimes in the U.S. The majority of justifiable killings are by law enforcement officers. According to the *Journal of the American Medical Association*, even when someone is home, a gun is used for protection in less than two percent of home-incursion crimes. Other nonfirearm options for protection against home incursion are available, such as dialing 911 (police will be dispatched even if you are not in a position to talk), buying a dog, or installing a burglar alarm system with monitoring by a protective services company.

On any given day, 1,100,000 Americans carry concealed weapons on them outside the workplace, and 2,100,000 in their vehicles. The rate is twice as high in the South as the rest of the nation. FBI data show that just 0.6% of violent-crime victims used a firearm in an attempt to defend themselves. According to the Bureau of Justice Statistics (BJS) National Crime Victimization Survey, 29% of violent-crime victims faced an offender with a gun. Of those, three percent suffered gunshot wounds. In other words, even if you are unfortunate enough to face an assailant with a firearm, there is a 97% chance that you will not be shot. BJS surveys from a number of years consistently indicate that about 85,000 crime victims use guns in an attempt to protect themselves or their property out of a total of 13,000,000 reported crimes (FBI) or 40,000,000 crimes, including unreported ones (Justice Department). Either way, guns are used in defense in less than one percent of crimes committed.

Defensive Gun Use Is Rare

The BJS victim interviews reveal that, in 72% of violent crimes, victims take some self-protective measures, but more than 98% of those acts do not include the use of a firearm. For instance, in 10% of cases, the victim attacked the perpetrator without using a weapon; nine percent scared off the offender; nine percent got help or sounded an alarm; 16% ran or hid; 13% persuaded or appeased the offender; 2.4% screamed; 1.7% threatened the offender with a weapon; and 1.5% threatened the offender without a weapon. Clearly, self-preservation methods without the use or threat of use of a weapon comprise the vast majority of cases. Sixty-five percent of those who employed some type of self-preservation method said their actions either helped avoid injury, scared off the offender, and/or enabled them to escape the situation or protect their property. Just nine percent of those who took self-protective measures said those actions made the situation worse.

There have been some gun ownership advocates who have exaggerated the extent by which ordinary citizens protect their lives and property with firearms. One widely quoted concealed weapons study concluded that violent-crime incidents declined in states that had passed right-to-carry (concealed weapons) laws. The full truth is that violent crime has decreased in every region of the country, regardless of gun ownership laws. FBI crime data indicates that, in the seven states that the NRA [National Rifle Association] identifies as having the most-restrictive concealed weapons laws on the books, homicides/non-negligent manslaughter declined in six of them between 1993 and 1999—Illinois, Kansas, Missouri, Nebraska, Ohio, and Wisconsin. The 11 states identified as having moderately restrictive concealed weapons laws all experienced homicide declines. For example, per 100,000 inhabitants, Missouri declined from 11.3 to 6.6; Ohio, from six to 3.5; and California and New York both experienced dramatic declines from approximately 13 to six and five, respectively.

U.S. homicide rates historically have been characterized by wide fluctuations, being relatively high in the 1920s and 1930s, much lower in the 1940s and 1950s, and then high again for much of the last half-century, although showing favorable declines in recent years. For every time a citizen used a firearm in a justifiable homicide, 131 lives were ended

Guns Increase the Lethality of Crime

A National Rifle Association bumper sticker states, "Guns don't kill people, people kill people." Strictly speaking, the slogan is incontrovertible. But so too is the observation that "people kill people" more frequently when guns are readily available. Gun assaults are far more likely to result in death than assaults with the next most deadly weapon, the knife. And guns are the instrument of death in 7 out of 10 homicides in the United States, a figure that is unparalleled among industrial democracies.

These facts help to explain the high rate of lethal violence in the United States. In 1992, assaults in New York were 11 times more likely to result in death than assaults in London. This difference is largely a consequence of the higher propensity of New Yorkers to attack one another with firearms. Whereas New York residents were as likely to attack one another with a gun as with a knife, Londoners were six times more likely to use a knife. If New Yorkers had assaulted one another with the same mix of weapons as Londoners, the number of deaths resulting from assault would have been about one third the actual death from the assault figure of 2,152. The greater availability of guns in the United States also means that robberies are more likely to result in death. In 1992, the overall "death rate" for gun robberies in New York was 8.4 per 1,000, about 10 times greater than the death rate for non-gun robberies. If the 91,000 New York City robberies in that year had resulted in death at the non-gun death rate, 79 New Yorkers would have lost their lives in the course of a robbery. The actual number of deaths from robberies was 357. . . .

According to recent estimates, there are about 200 million guns, including 70 million handguns, in circulation in the United States. The proportion of households possessing a firearm has remained stable at about 50% over the past three decades, but the percentage of households with a handgun has increased from 13% in 1959 to about 25% today. The United States now has more federally licensed gun dealers than gas stations. . . . In the United States, guns are quite literally everywhere, and their contribution to the country's extraordinary rate of killing is clear.

Katherine Beckett and Theodore Sasson, *The Politics of Injustice: Crime and Punishment in America*. Thousand Oaks, CA: Pine Forge Press, 2000.

in a firearm murder, suicide, or unintentional shooting. Law enforcement statistics and interviews show that approximately 45% of homicides were perpetrated by assailants related to or acquainted with their victim. Fifty-six percent of gun homicides resulted from arguments. Of all violent crime, 23% of offenders were family members and 48% acquaintances. Situations of family strife with the potential for domestic violence is a factor that should be kept in mind by any prospective gun owner.

Gun Ownership and Suicide

Gun ownership also has a correlation with suicide. According to the National Institutes of Mental Health, 19,000,000 Americans suffer some form of depression each year, with up to 20% of untreated cases choosing suicide. While there are other developed countries without high gun ownership with suicide rates higher than the U.S., firearms are the most lethal choice of suicide options. According to Physicians for Social Responsibility, 84 people die every day in America by suicide, and 50 of those are by firearms. The risk of suicide is five times greater in households with guns.

The 1994 Police Foundation Survey revealed that the average gun owner had had his or her firearm for 13 years. When evaluating a gun purchase, prospective buyers should consider the length of time they will own their gun in the context of the normal ups and downs that people face over the course of many years, including depression over a job loss or loved one, family fights, divorce, or a bout with alcohol and/or drugs.

There is an additional risk of teen suicide in homes with firearms and, according to the Surgeon General, five percent of youngsters between the ages of nine and 17 have a diagnosis of a major depression, with 10–15% having some symptoms of depression. Suicidal adolescents are 75 times more likely to commit suicide when a gun is kept in the home. Impulsiveness appears to play an important role in suicide, especially youth suicide. It is not uncommon for adolescents to have passing suicidal tendencies. Youth who attempt suicide rarely have a clear and sustained desire to die.

One of Many Factors

Guns, of course, are not the sole reason for violent crime and suicide in the U.S. Many experts agree that gun violence results from intertwined complex causes, such as family problems, neighborhood concerns, drug/alcohol abuse, media gun violence, school/work pressures, poverty, and accessibility to guns. Some have pointed to the fact that America is a heterogeneous society compared to others with lower rates of violence. However, the fact remains that 94% of black murders in the U.S. were by black offenders, and 87% of white murders were by white offenders. Special attention must be given to violence among blacks. Although African-Americans make up 12% of the population, 47% of all murder victims are black. According to FBI data, 35% of murder offenders were white, 35% black, and 28% unknown. Poverty and low education also have a correlation with violent crime.

A comparison between Department of Commerce statistics and FBI Uniform Crime Report data on murder and non-negligent manslaughter shows that states with lower-than-average high school graduation rates and lower-than-average per capita income consistently have higher homicide rates. A number of southern states bear these characteristics, and, when combined with a high percentage of gun ownership, there is an increase in the propensity for violence with fatal consequences.

Violence-reduction policies must be multi-faceted and include better education, domestic violence reduction, improvement of the plight of the urban poor, the cutting of drug/alcohol abuse (35% of violent crime victims said the perpetrator had been drinking), early mental health intervention, and increased parental involvement with children. Guns should not be viewed as the sole cause of violence, but as an important contributing factor. While there are other weapons used in violent crimes, guns are used in 65% of homicides and 59% of all suicides. Guns create a distance from the violent act compared to other weapons/actions, such as knives, strangulation, beatings, or use of blunt objects, which are visibly more violent and sometimes riskier for the perpetrator. It is simply too easy in today's society to pull the trigger to end a temporary episode of depression or rage.

Controlling Guns

It is within America's power to start moving toward a more rational approach to firearms. Gun-control proposals often include the following elements:

- Raising the legal age for the possession of handguns from 18 to 21
- Limiting handgun purchases so that no individual is able to buy more than one gun per month
- Holding parents legally accountable when their children commit crimes with guns that they obtained as a result of the negligent storage of the weapons and ammunition
- Improving the design and manufacture of firearms, including installing child-locks, personalizing a gun so that it can only be fired by its owner, and adding load indicators that tell the user that the gun is still loaded or magazine-disconnect safeties which prevent the gun from firing if the ammunition magazine is removed
- Applying restrictions on gun manufacturers who produce low-quality, easily concealable "junk guns" or Saturday night specials and strict regulations against cop-killer bullets and mail-order parts that allow individuals to assemble untraceable guns
- Educating consumers about the true risks and rewards of gun ownership for enhanced personal safety
- Prohibiting gun advertisements in publications with substantial youth readership and including warnings about the risks of guns in the home
- Altering distribution and sales practices by improving security systems to avoid theft from dealers, prohibiting straw purchases by gun traffickers who then resell guns on the streets to criminals, closing gun show loopholes, and legislating mandatory waiting periods
- Federal licensing of handgun owners and registration of the handguns.

Licensing of handgun owners and registration of the handgun itself deserves special mention, as it has been the cornerstone of handgun responsibility and accountability throughout most of the developed world. . . .

Some of the common components of licensing and registration in developed nations are reviewing criminal history, domestic violence, and mental health; gun owner training, including public safety education as a condition of licensing; demonstrated need for a handgun; club membership with regular attendance required, such as an approved pistol club; interviewing the applicant's current or most recent spouse; secure storage requirements with the handgun and ammunition stored separately; verification of storage through physical inspections; fraud-resistant licensing procedures, such as requiring a thumbprint or photograph; limitations on ammunition that can be purchased for the type of firearm declared; mandatory removal of firearms within 24 hours of a domestic protection order; and regular reviews of gun owners for reapplication and periodic interviews. . . .

It is time not to prohibit law-abiding citizens from owning a gun, but to be sure that they have correct factual data so that each can make an intelligent, informed choice pertaining to firearm ownership and then act responsibly after the purchase. Public policy should be geared to keeping firearms out of the hands of youth and to provide tools to trace firearms used in crimes to the original sources who are illegally providing firearms to criminals and young people. Continued tough enforcement of laws governing the use of firearms in the commission of a crime, coupled with a rational policy for law-abiding Americans, would be a major step in the right direction. In the area of gun policy, it is time to learn from the experiences of other developed nations in a manner that preserves individual rights, improves informed consumer choice, and encourages responsibility and accountability.

Periodical Bibliography

The following articles have been selected to supplement the diverse views presented in this chapter.

Sarah Brady and John R. Lott Jr.	"Would New Requirements for Gun Buyers Save Lives?" *Insight on the News*, June 21, 1999.
Business Week	"Say Yes to Serious Gun Control," August 16, 1999.
Fox Butterfield	"FBI Study Finds Gun Use in Violent Crimes Declining," *New York Times*, October 18, 1999.
Congressional Digest	"Firearms in America: The Link Between Guns and Violence," November 1999.
Richard F. Corlin	"The Secrets of Gun Violence in America," *Vital Speeches of the Day*, August 1, 2001.
Economist	"Economic Focus: Gun Control and Crime," January 13, 2001.
David Kopel	"An Army of Gun Lies," *National Review*, April 17, 2000.
Erik Larson	"Squeezing Out the Bad Guys: How the ATF and Local Police Have Dramatically Turned the Tide in the Battle Against Crime and Guns," *Time*, August 9, 1999.
John R. Lott Jr.	"When Gun Control Costs Lives," *National Forum*, Fall 2000.
Joyce Lee Malcolm	"Gun Control's Twisted Outcome: Restricting Firearms Has Helped Make England More Crime-Ridden than the U.S.," *Reason*, November 2002.
Mark Mazzetti	"Taking a (Gun) Powder?" *Newsweek*, May 7, 2001.
Noam Scheiber	"Gun Shy," *New Republic*, January 29, 2001.
Jacob Sullum and Michael W. Lynch	"Cold Comfort," *Reason*, January 2000.
Woody West	"U.S. Gun Control Laws Don't Save Lives," *Insight on the News*, November 10, 2003.

CHAPTER 3

How Should the Criminal Justice System Be Reformed?

Chapter Preface

The popularity of "tough-on-crime" policies is nothing new in American politics. Since the 1970s, the general trend in the United States has been toward longer prison sentences for most types of crimes. In 1970 there were just under 200,000 people being held in the U.S. prison system; in 1980 there were just over 315,000; in 1990 there were almost 740,000; and by 2000 there were over 1.3 million. To accommodate such a dramatic increase in convicts, since 1980, about one thousand new prisons and jails have been built in the United States.

One type of "tough-on-crime" policy that has contributed to the increase in prisoners is mandatory minimum sentences. Congress passed more than twenty mandatory sentencing laws between 1985 and 1991—most of them for drug offenses—and most states followed suit. For example, in 2000 in Massachusetts, conviction for possession of two hundred grams of cocaine mandated a fifteen-year prison sentence.

In principle, mandatory sentences are intended to "send a message" to criminals that particular offenses will be severely punished and to ensure that judges do not have the authority to hand out overly lenient sentences for particular types of crimes. In practice, mandatory minimums have resulted in more prisoners serving longer terms.

Many critics object to mandatory-minimum laws on the grounds that they override judges' authority to adjust sentences on a case-by-case basis. But it may be issues of finance rather than fairness that put an end to mandatory minimums. In the face of budget deficits and expensive, overcrowded prisons, many states have begun scaling back their mandatory-minimum laws. Michigan, for example, has repealed its mandatory-minimum laws and returned sentencing discretion to judges. The state expects to save an estimated $41 million from the reforms in 2003. Dozens of other states are following suit, scaling back penalties for low-level, nonviolent offenses.

The rise and fall of mandatory minimums demonstrate the enormous challenge that reformers face in trying to make the criminal justice system fair, effective, and fiscally sound. The authors in the following chapter debate some of the most high-profile issues facing the criminal justice system.

"America has overtaken Russia as the world's most aggressive jailer."

America's Prison System Needs to Be Reformed

The *Economist*

The *Economist* is a weekly magazine of business and politics. The editors of the *Economist* argue in the following viewpoint that America's high incarceration rates are a symptom of serious flaws in the U.S. criminal justice system. Harsh, inflexible sentencing guidelines have resulted in thousands of individuals being locked up for years for relatively minor crimes, with little possibility of parole. The *Economist* also emphasizes how ineffective prison is in reforming criminals: The lack of rehabilitation programs within prisons and the social discrimination that ex-convicts face after returning to normal life makes it very likely that released prisoners will return to a life of crime. Clearly, the editors of the *Economist* write, the U.S. prison system is in need of serious reform.

As you read, consider the following questions:

1. What proportion of black men have served time in prison, according to the *Economist*?
2. What proportion of released prisoners are rearrested within three years of release, according to the viewpoint?
3. What percentage of Americans have lost their voting rights as a result of their criminal record, as stated by the authors?

At the end of August [2002], Mike, a 31-year-old Latino from Chicago's south side, will walk away from prison a free man. Again. This is his second long prison term for dealing in drugs and stealing cars; he has been in and out of jail a dozen times. He will be released into the same community where he has found trouble so many times before; he will attempt to reunite with his five children born to several different mothers. "Nothing really scares me about leaving," says Mike. "It's just the thought of coming back."

America's incarceration rate was roughly constant from 1925 to 1973, with an average of 110 people behind bars for every 100,000 residents. By 2000, however, the rate of incarceration in state and federal prisons had more than quadrupled, to 478. America has overtaken Russia as the world's most aggressive jailer. When local jails are included in the American tally, the United States locks up nearly 700 people per 100,000, compared with 102 for Canada, 132 for England and Wales, 85 for France and a paltry 48 in Japan. Roughly 2m [million] Americans are currently behind bars, with some 4.5m on parole or on probation (the probationers are on suspended sentences). Another 3m Americans are ex-convicts who have served their sentences and are no longer under the control of the justice system.

Christopher Uggen and Melissa Thompson, sociologists at the University of Minnesota, and Jeff Manza, a sociologist at Northwestern University near Chicago, have done rough calculations suggesting that some 13m Americans—7% of the adult population and nearly 12% of the men—have been found guilty of a serious crime. Not all of these have been behind bars but, legally speaking, the felony conviction is the crucial distinction. American job applicants are asked whether they have been convicted of a felony, not whether they have served time. And the figures for some parts of the population are much higher than the overall averages. Roughly one in five black men has been incarcerated at some point in his life; one in three has been convicted of a felony.

How Did It Happen?

The imprisonment rate is tied to the crime rate. America has a high number of violent criminals, particularly those who use guns; America's homicide rate is five to seven times higher than the rate in most industrialised countries, according to Marc Mauer of the Sentencing Project in Washington, DC.

But America is also "tough on crime". For similar offences, an American convict is more likely to go to prison and to draw a longer sentence than his European peer. America has taken a particularly punitive approach to its drugs problem. The incarceration rate for drug offences was 15 inmates per 100,000 adults in 1980; by 1996, it was 148 inmates per 100,000 adults.

This keenness to lock people up is matched by a complete lack of interest in them when they get out. Which they do—and faster than you might think. The average prison sentence is still only 28 months. Two-fifths of state prisoners will be released in the next 12 months.

The typical inmate goes into prison disadvantaged by almost every measure. He is more likely than other Americans to be poor and poorly educated, to have a sorry employment record, to be a junkie, to be mentally ill, and to be a member of a minority group. A survey of Californian inmates found that half were functionally illiterate. Prison could fix some of those social disadvantages; usually it does not. So the typical inmate is released from prison with all the problems he went in with—plus a prison record that makes finding a job or a place to live even harder.

When inmates walk away from a state prison in Illinois, they are given $10, a set of street clothes and a one-way bus or train ticket to some approved destination. They leave the structured environment of prison, in which they are at least guaranteed a bed, meals and basic health care, and return to a world full of temptations, often to the very neighbourhood in which they first fell foul of the law.

Charles, a boyish-looking 25-year-old who has spent three-and-a-half years in prison for guns and drugs offences, will be released this year [2002]. He worries both about his old friends, who have not mended their ways, and his old enemies, who may still have scores to settle. "There's people who left here and got killed the first day," he says.

A survey of employers in five large cities found that 65% would not knowingly hire an ex-convict. Many would not be allowed to do so legally anyway. Another facet of the "tough on crime" movement has been to exclude ex-convicts from certain kinds of employment. In Illinois, ex-felons are banned from some 57 different professions, including such jobs as manicurist and barber, says Diane Williams, president of Chicago's Safer Foundation, a non-profit organisation that helps ex-offenders.

Ex-convicts, whose families are often less than enthusiastic about their return, can also be excluded from public housing. Three-quarters of inmates leaving prison have been on drugs; one in five has a mental illness. It should be no surprise that ex-inmates have high rates of unemployment and homelessness.

Doing Time

The sentencing laws also skew the system in another way. Sentences used to be indeterminate: a man might get five to 20 years, with a parole board deciding when he was to be released. In the mid-1970s, three in four American prisoners were released only after appearing before a parole board. This process annoyed both left-wingers, who complained that it was racially biased, and conservatives, who objected to letting prisoners out "early". Now only 30% of prisoners appear before parole boards; the rest are released when they have done their time, whether they are prepared for life outside or not.

Of course, most of these people are released conditionally, usually for a period of parole in which they must live by certain rules (such as staying off drugs). But nowadays a typical parole officer may be responsible for 50% more people on parole than he was in the 1970s. Methods of broad surveillance, such as drug testing, have replaced more personal support and supervision. An ex-offender may have only a few short meetings with his parole officer each month. "The philosophy of the parole unit has changed," says Jerry Butler, who joined the Safer Foundation after 31 years in the Illinois Department of Corrections. "Now they all have cars, guns, bullet-proof vests and badges."

Unsurprisingly, more inmates are failing their first big test outside prison. In 1985, 70% of people on parole successfully completed their term; by 1999, only 42% did. Those who break their parole now account for a third of prison admissions, the fastest-growing category.

Altogether, roughly two-thirds of released prisoners are rearrested within three years of release; 40% are already back in prison in that time. And those are just the ones who get caught. "If you return the guy to the community with $10 and a suit of clothes and no support systems, you can just about guarantee that that person is going to resort to some kind of criminal behaviour," says Mr Butler. And the crimes the ex-inmate commits could well be nasty ones: one in four prisoners is a violent offender.

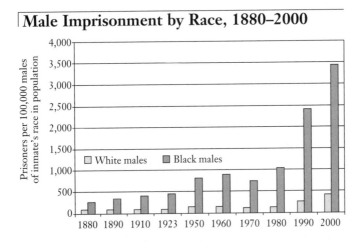

Male Imprisonment by Race, 1880–2000

Prisoners per 100,000 males of inmate's race in population

□ White males ■ Black males

1880 1890 1910 1923 1950 1960 1970 1980 1990 2000

Henry Ruth and Kevin R. Reitz, *The Challenge of Crime: Rethinking Our Response*. Cambridge, MA: Harvard University Press, 2003.

The effect of all these ex-prisoners is beginning to be felt. Inevitably, it is disproportionately large in certain areas. A study of Cleveland, Ohio, for example, found that 3% of the city's neighbourhoods were home to 20% of the state's ex-prisoners.

"They come back with their own baggage," says Jeffrey Fagan, a professor of law and public health at Columbia University. They also come back dangerously ill in many cases. In 1997, a quarter of the people living with HIV or AIDS in the United States had come out of prison that year. The numbers are even higher for hepatitis C and tuberculosis. When a resistant form of TB hit New York city in the late 1980s, 80% of cases were traced to prisons.

America's huge criminal class also has profound political implications. Most states limit the voting rights of felons and ex-felons. As a result, 4.7m Americans, or 2.3% of the voting population, have lost their rights. The figure is nearly 7% in Alabama. One in six black men cannot vote in Virginia and Kentucky. This causes alienation, and changes elections. Felons may not be enthusiastic voters, but they vote overwhelmingly for Democrats. Messrs Uggen and Manza have calculated that if felons had been able to vote in Florida, [Democrat] Al Gore would be president [instead of Republican George W. Bush].

In Praise of Rehab

The notion of rehabilitating prisoners went out of vogue in the 1970s, when research seemed to show that prison programmes had no effect on recidivism. New research suggests the opposite.

For example, a study of residential drug treatment within federal prisons showed that inmates who completed the programme were 73% less likely to be rearrested than those who had not completed it. Such programmes are being curtailed just as research is beginning to show they work. In 1991, one in four state-prison inmates received treatment for drug addiction; by 1997 it was one in ten. Prison-based job-education programmes have also been shown to reduce recidivism, but fewer prisoners than before now take part in them.

Jeremy Travis, a senior fellow at the Urban Institute, proposes an improved version of the old parole board in which an offender's "re-entry management" would be assigned to the judge who sentenced him to prison in the first place. The judge would oversee a plan that would include paying restitution to the victim. He would monitor the offender's participation in relevant programmes and punish failure. Drug treatment inside prison could be linked to post-prison treatment outside. Similarly, job training in prison might be co-ordinated with work after release.

Mike and Charles are relatively lucky, as prisoners go. They are finishing their prison terms at the Crossroads Community Correctional Centre, a "transitional facility" operated by the Safer Foundation for the state of Illinois. They are enrolled in an intensive drug-treatment programme, taught about matters such as parenting and given housing assistance before release. Mike leaves the facility by day to work at a bakery; Charles works at a fast-food restaurant. Both are required to save a portion of their wages.

Will it make any difference? "There is no guarantee," admits Mr Butler. Would-be helpers face a stunning paucity of data on what distinguishes successful ex-prisoners, but offenders who have been through the Safer Foundation are 40% less likely to be rearrested.

There are two straws to grasp. First, politicians are beginning to notice the problem. The Justice Department has recently allocated $100m in grants to help prisoners on release—a start, though not much against the $54 billion a year that America spends on its whole prison system.

Second, a few Americans are beginning to reconsider the war on drugs. A 1997 RAND study concluded that spending money to reduce drug consumption through treatment rather than incarceration would reduce serious crime 15 times more effectively. In November 2000, California's voters passed Proposition 36, which sends first- and second-time non-violent drug offenders to treatment rather than prison.

Conwanis, a 26-year-old black man with two children, will leave prison in October [2002] after serving a three-year sentence for drug and guns offences. He failed to graduate from high school, and he also failed a high-school equivalency exam in prison that would have earned him a diploma. But he is clean of drugs (with tests to prove it) and he has been working 12-hour shifts in a transitional job at a Country Kitchen restaurant. "I can't continue to come in and out of jail," he says. It would be better for everyone if he made something more of his life this time.

| *"Keeping known criminals locked up is a sensible and effective crime policy."*

America's Prison System Is Effective at Controlling Crime

Jeff Jacoby

In the following viewpoint Jeff Jacoby contends that America's prison system is largely responsible for the drop in crime that the United States has been experiencing since 1993. Jacoby acknowledges that America has much higher incarceration rates than other countries, but he also points out that while crime rates in the United States have been dropping, they have been rising in many other countries. Jacoby also maintains that the high cost of keeping over 2 million people in prison is balanced by the benefits accrued from low crime rates. Jacoby is a columnist for the *Boston Globe*.

As you read, consider the following questions:
1. By how much did the violent crime rate drop from 1993 to 2002, according to Jacoby?
2. What figures does the author provide to support his claim that releasing criminals costs society more than keeping them in prison?
3. What are some of the countries that the author points to as having rising crime rates?

Major crime in the United States is at a 30-year-low, and the *Christian Science Monitor* can't understand it.

In a story this week [August 25, 2003] headlined "A drop in violent crime that's hard to explain," the *Monitor*'s Alexandra Marks reported on the latest data from the Bureau of Justice Statistics, an agency of the US Justice Department. According to the bureau, there were 23 million instances of violent and property crime last year—48 percent fewer than the 44 million recorded in 1973. (The numbers don't include murder, which is measured separately by the FBI.) In just the past 10 years, the violent crime rate has plummeted by a stunning 54 percent, from 50 crimes per 1,000 US residents in 1993 to 23 per 1,000 in 2002.

The plunge in serious crime is pervasive; it crosses racial, ethnic, and gender lines and shows up in every income group and region. But welcome as they are, the new data are only the latest extension of a downward trend that first appeared in the 1980s, not long after the nationwide crackdown on crime got underway. The dramatic drop in criminal activity followed an equally dramatic boom in prison construction and a sharp surge in incarceration rates. The conclusion is obvious: Stricter punishment has led to lower crime.

But it isn't obvious to the *Monitor*. Marks's story makes no mention of prisons or prisoners. It claims that criminologists are actually "quick to list the reasons" why crime should be going *up*, such as the soft economy, cuts in local government spending, and the diversion of police from walking neighborhood beats to guarding public facilities against terror.

The only explanation Marks can offer for the continuing reduction in crime comes from Alfred Blumstein of Carnegie Mellon University, who speculates that [after the September 11, 2001, terrorist attacks], Americans may be treating each other more considerately. "The only thing I can think of," Blumstein says, "is some sense of cohesion that's emerging as a result of the terrorist threat."

To be fair, Marks and the *Monitor* aren't the only ones with a blind spot for the nexis between crime and punishment. In the Associated Press story on the Justice Department data, there is no mention of incarceration until the 11th paragraph. "Some criminologists," the AP grudgingly notes, "say tougher prison sentences and more prisons are key factors."

None of those criminologists is quoted; instead, the point is dismissed as "political rhetoric" by the Justice Policy Institute, an anti-imprisonment advocacy group.

Imprisoning Criminals Reduces Crime

No one disputes that more criminals are being locked up in this country or that they are spending more time behind bars. The Justice Department reported in July [2003] that the nation's prison population had reached an all-time high of 2.1 million in 2002, with violent criminals accounting for most of the increase. At year's end, 1 of every 143 US residents was in a state or federal prison or jail.

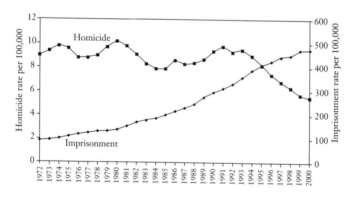

Incarceration Growth and Homicide Reduction

Henry Ruth and Kevin R. Reitz, *The Challenge of Crime: Rethinking Our Response*. Cambridge, MA: Harvard University Press, 2003.

That is a much higher level of imprisonment than is found in other modern democracies, a fact liberal critics point to as evidence of American vengefulness. "The price of imprisoning so many Americans is too high . . . 5 to 10 times as high as in many other industrialized nations," admonished the *New York Times* in a recent editorial. "Locking the door and throwing away the key may make for good campaign sound bites, but it is a costly and inhumane crime policy."

Actually, keeping known criminals locked up is a sensible and effective crime policy. The *Times* laments that it costs $22,000 per year to keep each inmate in custody, but that is not an exorbitant price for preventing millions of annual murders, rapes, armed robberies, and assaults. The cost to society of a single armed robbery has been estimated at more than $50,000; multiply that by the 12 or 13 attacks the average released prisoner commits per year, and $22,000 per inmate looks like quite a bargain.

While crime has been tumbling in the United States, it has been soaring elsewhere. "Crime has recently hit record highs in Paris, Madrid, Stockholm, Amsterdam, Toronto, and a host of other major cities," Eli Lehrer wrote in the *Weekly Standard* [in 2002]. "In a 2001 study, the British Home Office found violent and property crime increased in the late 1990s in every wealthy country except the United States. American property crime rates have been lower than those in Britain, Canada, and France since the early 1990s, and violent crime rates in the European Union, Australia, and Canada have recently begun to equal and even surpass those in the United States. Even Sweden, once the epitome of cosmopolitan socialist prosperity, now has a crime victimization rate 20 percent higher than the United States."

Not every inmate belongs in prison. Petty drug offenders, for example, are better suited to intense probation and treatment than to jail. But on the whole, America's policy of locking up large numbers of criminals for long terms is doing just what it was meant to do: making us safer. Maybe the Europeans should follow suit.

"Most conservatives who support racial profiling . . . consider [it] an essential ingredient of effective law enforcement. But it isn't."

Law Enforcement Agencies Should Eliminate Racial Profiling

James B. Forman Jr.

In the following viewpoint James B. Forman Jr. argues that blacks are much more likely than whites to be stopped, searched, and harassed by police. Forman writes that liberal leaders have decried racial profiling, and he argues that conservative leaders, who are more inclined to defend police tactics, should also reject racial profiling because it undermines both effective policing and the Constitution's guarantee of equal treatment under the law. Forman contends that racial profiling pits the police against black communities, when instead police should view communities as partners in crime-reduction efforts. Forman is a fellow at the New America Foundation in Washington, D.C., and chair of the Maya Angelou Public Charter Board of Trustees.

As you read, consider the following questions:
1. What findings from a study of Maryland police searches does the author use to show the prevalence of racial profiling?
2. In the author's opinion, why do most conservatives support racial profiling?
3. In Forman's view, what are the two main ways in which racial profiling makes law enforcement less effective?

The Maya Angelou Public Charter School in Washington, D.C., is the kind of institution conservatives love—a place that offers opportunity but demands responsibility. Students are in school ten and a half hours per day, all year long, mostly studying core subjects like reading, writing, math, and history. When not in class, they work in student-run businesses, where they earn money and learn job skills. Those who achieve academically are held in high esteem not only by their teachers but by their peers. Those who disrupt class or otherwise violate the rules are subject to punishment, including expulsion, as determined by a panel of students and teachers.

The results have been impressive. Most Maya Angelou students had academic difficulty at their previous schools. In fact, more than one-half had stopped even attending school on a regular basis before they came to Maya Angelou, while more than one-third had been in the juvenile court system. Yet more than 90 percent of its graduates go on to college, compared with a citywide rate of just 50 percent. This success stems in part from the school's small classes, innovative curriculum, and dedicated staff. But it is also due to its fundamentally conservative ethos: If you work hard and don't make excuses, society will give you a chance, no matter what your background is.

I can speak to this with some authority because I helped establish the school four years ago and still teach an elective there today. But, for all the school's accomplishments, we keep running up against one particularly debilitating problem. It's awfully hard to convince poor, African American kids that discrimination isn't an obstacle, that authority must be respected, and that individual identity matters more than racial identity when experiences beyond school walls repeatedly contradict it. And that's precisely what's happening today thanks to a policy many conservatives condone: Racial profiling by the police.

The Prevalence of Racial Profiling

The prevalence of racial profiling is no secret. Numerous statistical studies have shown that being black substantially raises the odds of a person being stopped and searched by

129

the police—even though blacks who are stopped are no more likely than whites to be carrying drugs. As David Cole and John Lamberth recently pointed out in the *New York Times*, in Maryland "73 percent of those stopped and searched on a section of Interstate 95 were black, yet state police reported that equal percentages of the whites and blacks who were searched, statewide, had drugs or other contraband." Blacks were actually far less likely than whites to be found carrying drugs in New Jersey, a state whose police force has acknowledged the use of racial profiling. According to Cole and Lamberth, consensual searches "yielded contraband, mostly drugs, on 25 percent of whites, 13 percent of blacks and only 5 percent of Latinos."

Behind these statistics are hundreds if not thousands of well-chronicled anecdotes, some from America's most prominent black citizens. Erroll McDonald, vice president and executive editor of Pantheon publishing, was driving a rented Jaguar in New Orleans when he was stopped—simply "to show cause why I shouldn't be deemed a problematic Negro in a possibly stolen car." Wynton Marsalis says, "Shit, the police slapped me upside the head when I was in high school. I wasn't Wynton Marsalis then. I was just another nigger standing out somewhere on the street whose head could be slapped and did get slapped."

Even off-duty black police frequently tell of being harassed by their unsuspecting white colleagues. Consider the case of Robert Byrd, an eleven-year veteran of the D.C. police, who was off duty and out of uniform when he tried to stop a carjacking and robbery in Southeast Washington last March [2001]. After witnessing the crime, Byrd used his police radio to alert a police dispatcher, then followed the stolen van in his own. Byrd got out of his van as marked police vehicles arrived. According to Byrd, white officers then began beating him in the belief that he was the African American suspect. The real perpetrators were caught later that night.

None of these stories would surprise the students at Maya Angelou. Almost weekly this past spring [2001], officers arrived at the corner of 9th and T Streets NW (in front of our school), threw our students against the wall, and searched them. As you might imagine, these are not polite encounters. They are an aggressive show of force in which children are required to "assume the position": legs spread, face against the wall or squad car, hands behind the head. Police officers then search them, feeling every area of their bodies. Last spring, a police officer chased one male student into the school, wrestled him to the ground, then drew his gun. Another time, when a student refused a police request to leave the corner in front of our school (where the student was taking a short break between classes, in complete compliance with school rules and D.C. law), the officer grabbed him, cuffed him, and started putting him into a police van, before a school official intervened. These students committed no crime other than standing outside a school in a high-drug-use neighborhood. Indeed, despite the numerous searches, no drugs have ever been discovered, and no student has ever been found in violation of the law.

Liberals generally decry such incidents; conservatives generally deny that they take place. "The racial profiling we're all supposed to be outraged about doesn't actually happen very much," explained Jonah Goldberg in his *National Review Online* column last spring. And even those conservatives who admit the practice's frequency often still insist it does more good than harm. "The evidence suggests," William Tucker wrote in a recent issue of the *Weekly Standard*, "that racial profiling is an effective law enforcement tool, though it undeniably visits indignity on the innocent."

The Conservative Case Against Racial Profiling

In other words, liberals—who are generally more concerned about individual rights and institutionalized racism—believe racial profiling contradicts their principles. Conservatives, on the other hand—who tolerate greater invasions of privacy in the name of law and order—consider racial profiling to be generally consistent with theirs. But conservatives are wrong—racial profiling profoundly violates core conservative principles.

It is conservatives, after all, who remind us that government policy doesn't affect only resources; it affects values, which in turn affect people's behavior. This argument was at the heart of the conservative critique of welfare policy. For years, conservatives (along with some liberals) argued that welfare policies—like subsidizing unmarried, unemployed women with children—fostered a culture of dependency. Only by demanding that citizens take responsibility for their own fates, the argument went, could government effectively combat poverty.

The Evidence for Racial Profiling

Although some observers claim that racial profiling doesn't exist, there is an abundance of stories and statistics that document the practice. One case where law enforcement officers were particularly bold in their declaration of intent involved U.S. Forest Service officers in California's Mendocino National Forest [in 2000]. In an attempt to stop marijuana growing, forest rangers were told to question all Hispanics whose cars were stopped, regardless of whether pot was actually found in their vehicles. Tim Crews, the publisher of the *Sacramento Valley Mirror*, a biweekly newspaper, published a memo he'd gotten from a federal law enforcement officer. The memo told park rangers "to develop probable cause for stop . . . if a vehicle stop is conducted and no marijuana is located and the vehicle has Hispanics inside, at a minimum we would like all individuals FI'd [field interrogated]." A spokeswoman for Mendocino National Forest called the directive an "unfortunate use of words."

The statistics are equally telling. Consider *Crises of the Anti-Drug Effort, 1999*, a report by Chad Thevenot of the Criminal Justice Policy Foundation, a group that monitors abuses of the American legal system. Thevenot writes: "76 percent of the motorists stopped along a 50-mile stretch of I-95 by Maryland's Special Traffic Interdiction Force (STIF) were black, according to an Associated Press computer analysis of car searches from January through September 1995. . . . Blacks constitute 25 percent of Maryland's population, and 20 percent of Marylanders with driver's licenses." . . . One state police investigator testified that 94 percent of the motorists stopped in one town were minorities.

Gene Callahan and William Anderson, "The Roots of Racial Profiling," *Reason*, August/September 2001.

But if sending out welfare checks with no strings attached sends the wrong message, so does racial profiling. For the conservative ethos about work and responsibility to resonate, black citizens must believe they are treated the same way as white citizens—that with equal responsibilities go equal rights. In *The Dream and the Nightmare*, which President [George W.] Bush cites as one of the most influential books he has ever read, the conservative theorist Myron Magnet writes: "What underclass kids need most . . . is an authoritative link to traditional values of work, study, and self-improvement, and the assurance that these values can permit them to claim full membership in the larger community." Magnet quotes Eugene Lange, a businessman who promised scholarships to inner-city kids who graduated from high school: "'It's important that [inner-city kids] grow up to recognize that they are not perpetuating a life of the pariah, but that the resources of the community are legitimately theirs to take advantage of and contribute to and be a part of.'"

Magnet is right. But random and degrading police searches radically undermine this message. They tell black kids that they are indeed pariahs—that, no matter how hard they study, they remain suspects. As one Maya Angelou first-year student explained to me: "We can be perfect, perfect, doing everything right, and they still treat us like dogs. No, worse than dogs, because criminals are treated worse than dogs." Or, as a junior asked me, noting the discrepancy between the message delivered by the school and the message delivered by the police: "How can you tell us we can be anything if they treat us like we're nothing?"

Indeed, people like myself—teachers, counselors, parents—try desperately to convince these often jaded kids that hard work really will pay off. In so doing, we are quite consciously pursuing an educational approach that conservatives have long advocated. We are addressing what conservative criminologist James Q. Wilson calls "intangible problems—problems of 'values,'" the problems that sometimes make "blacks less likely to take advantage of opportunities." But we are constantly fighting other people in the neighborhood who tell kids that bourgeois norms of work, family, and sexuality are irrelevant and impossible. Since the state will forever treat you as an outlaw, they say, you might as well act like one. Every time police single out a young black man for harassment, those other people sound more credible—and we sound like dupes.

The Government Should Be Color-Blind

Then there's that other vaunted conservative ideal: color-blindness. In recent years, conservatives have argued relentlessly for placing less emphasis on race. Since discrimination is on the wane, they suggest, government itself must stop making race an issue—i.e., no more affirmative action in admissions, no more set-asides in contracting, no more tailoring of government programs to favor particular racial or ethnic groups. In the words of affirmative action critics Abigail and Stephen Thernstrom, it's essential to fight the "politics of racial grievance" and counter the "suspicion that nothing fundamental [has] changed." Society, says Magnet, "needs to tell [blacks] that they can do it—not that, because of past victimization, they cannot."

But it's hard to tell young black men that they are not victims because of their race when police routinely make them victims because of their race. Students at Maya Angelou are acutely aware that the police do not treat young people the same way at Sidwell Friends and St. Albans, schools for Washington's overwhelmingly white elite. As another Maya Angelou first-year told me, "You think they would try that stuff with white kids? Never." Such knowledge makes them highly suspicious of the conservative assertion that blacks should forego certain benefits—such as racial preferences in admissions—because of the moral value of color-blindness. Why, they wonder, aren't white people concerned about that principle when it hurts blacks as well as when it benefits them? And racial profiling makes them cynical about the conservative demand that blacks not see the world in racialized, group-identity terms. Why, they wonder, don't white people demand the same of the police?

Racial Profiling Is Counterproductive

Most conservatives who support racial profiling are not racist; they simply consider the practice an essential ingredient of effective law enforcement. But it isn't. Indeed, the great irony of conservative support for racial profiling is that conservative principles themselves explain why racial profiling actually makes law enforcement less effective.

For one thing, discriminatory police practices create unnecessary and unproductive hostility between police and the communities they serve. Imagine that you are 17, standing outside your school during a break from class, talking to friends, laughing, playing, and just relaxing. Imagine that squad cars pull up; officers jump out, shouting, guns drawn; and you are thrown against the wall, elbowed in the back, legs kicked apart, and violently searched. Your books are strewn on the ground. You ask what's going on, and you are told to "shut the fuck up" or you will be taken downtown. When it finally ends, the officers leave, giving no apology, no explanation, and you are left to fix your clothes, pick up your books, and gather your pride. Imagine that this is not the first time this has happened to you, that it has happened repeatedly, in one form or another, throughout your adolescence. Now imagine that, the day after the search, there is a crime in your neighborhood about which you hear a rumor. You know the police are looking for information, and you see one of the officers who searched you yesterday (or indeed any officer) asking questions about the crime. How likely are you to help?

Racial harassment hampers law enforcement in another, more subtle way as well: by reducing the stigma that law-abiding neighborhood residents attach to a person they see being detained by the police. For a community to be vigilant, it must have some idea of who is—and who isn't—a law-breaker. People generally take their cues on this from a variety of sources, including watching which people the police themselves stop and search. Then they keep a closer eye on those people themselves. But random police searches undermine that calculus. Many black people report that, when they see the police pulling over a car with a black driver or searching a black kid on the street, they don't ask: "What did that guy do?" They instead wonder: "Why is that cop harassing that guy?" The stigma of lawbreaking is weakened. Conservatives—usually the ones arguing for attaching more, not less, stigma to lawbreakers—ought to grasp this intuitively.

In fact, for all the conservative paeans to New York Mayor Rudy Giuliani, the data show that police forces that win the respect of high-crime communities reduce crime at least as much as those that simply bust heads. Look at San Diego.

During the 1990s San Diego police divided the city into small residential units. (According a local captain, "We basically threw out the original beat boundaries. We went to the community and said, 'Where do you think your neighborhood boundaries really begin and end?'") They assigned officers to those specific beats, engaged community leaders in an ongoing dialogue about how to solve various problems, and developed a corps of 1,200 citizen volunteers who became eyes and ears for the police.

Compare this to Giuliani's New York, which (particularly after the departure of Commissioner William Bratton, architect of the city's original police reform program) pursued an ultra-hard-line policy of "zero tolerance." That policy, as practiced by the city's now-notorious Street Crimes Unit, quickly became an invitation to hyperaggressive abuse. The Street Crimes Unit adopted "We Own the Night" as its motto, and some of its officers wore t-shirts emblazoned with the Hemingway quote: certainly there is no hunting like the hunting of man, and those who have hunted armed men long enough and liked it, never really care for anything else thereafter. It was a deliberately antagonistic posture, one that contributed to the attack on Abner Louima and to the killings of Amadou Diallo and Patrick Dorismond. And it has left many black New Yorkers profoundly alienated from the police officers who are meant to protect and serve them. In a 1998 Justice Department survey of citizen satisfaction with police in twelve American cities, San Diego's was the second-highest-rated force; New York's finished third to last.

But the important point for conservatives is that, for all the ill will they sowed, the New York police were no better at stopping crime than their San Diego counterparts. In fact, they were slightly worse. In testimony before the Senate Judiciary Committee, University of Toledo Law Professor David Harris said that "while homicide in New York fell 70.6 percent between 1991 and 1998. . . . San Diego's results were even more impressive . . . a fall of 76.4 percent, the best in the country." Statistics were similar for robbery: It fell 60 percent in New York but 63 percent in San Diego. And because they enjoyed more help from average citizens, says Harris, the San Diego police got those results with a much smaller force:

The city has just 1.7 officers per 1,000 residents, while New York has 5. In other words, smaller government—something else conservatives care about quite a bit.

Working with Communities

And San Diego's experience is not unique. As Heritage Foundation fellow Eli Lehrer has shown, cities that have instituted genuinely community-oriented approaches to policing have reduced crime while simultaneously developing stronger relationships with citizens. The most successful forces do not rely on ironfisted special units like New York's but rather invest in neighborhood patrols. When I brought up Lehrer's thesis to several Maya Angelou students, they found it self-evident. "What do you expect?" asked one. "We know who is doing right and who is doing wrong, and if they talked to us instead of jumping us, they might find out, too." Such words could be music to conservatives' ears—but only if they are willing to listen.

"If the police are now to be accused of racism every time that they go where the crime is, that's the end of public safety."

Racial Profiling Is a Myth

Heather MacDonald

Heather MacDonald is a contributing editor to *City Journal* and the author of *Are Cops Racist?* In the following viewpoint she argues that despite the outcry against racial profiling, there is little evidence that police engage in the practice. MacDonald writes that while it is wrong for police to stop or search individuals based solely on their race, it is permissible to use race as one of several factors in deciding whether to stop an individual, and this is the type of profiling used by police. MacDonald argues that the most famous report supposedly documenting extensive use of racial profiling is based on shoddy research. She warns that the crusade against racial profiling could result in an atmosphere in which police are penalized for making arrests in the neighborhoods where they are needed most.

As you read, consider the following questions:
1. What is the difference between "hard" and "soft" racial profiling, as explained by the author?
2. What does MacDonald say was the "most important victory of the anti–racial profiling agitators"?
3. By what percentage did drug arrests along New Jersey's Garden State Parkway drop in 2000, according to MacDonald?

Heather MacDonald, "The Myth of Racial Profiling," *City Journal*, vol. 11, Spring 2001. Copyright © 2001 by *City Journal*. Reproduced by permission.

The anti–"racial profiling" juggernaut must be stopped, before it obliterates the crime-fighting gains of the last decade, especially in inner cities. The anti-profiling crusade thrives on an ignorance of policing and a willful blindness to the demographics of crime. Yet politicians are swarming on board. In February [2001], President George W. Bush joined the rush, declaring portentously: "Racial profiling is wrong, and we will end it in America."

Too bad no one asked President Bush: "What exactly do you mean by 'racial profiling,' and what evidence do you have that it exists?" For the anti-profiling crusaders have created a headlong movement without defining their central term and without providing a shred of credible evidence that "racial profiling" is a widespread police practice.

The ultimate question in the profiling controversy is whether the disproportionate involvement of blacks and Hispanics with law enforcement reflects police racism or the consequences of disproportionate minority crime. Anti-profiling activists hope to make police racism an all but irrebuttable presumption whenever enforcement statistics show high rates of minority stops and arrests. But not so fast.

Two meanings of "racial profiling" intermingle in the activists' rhetoric. What we may call "hard" profiling uses race as the *only* factor in assessing criminal suspiciousness: an officer sees a black person and, without more to go on, pulls him over for a pat-down on the chance that he may be carrying drugs or weapons. "Soft" racial profiling is using race as one factor among others in gauging criminal suspiciousness: the highway police, for example, have intelligence that Jamaican drug posses with a fondness for Nissan Pathfinders are transporting marijuana along the northeast corridor. A New Jersey trooper sees a black motorist speeding in a Pathfinder and pulls him over in the hope of finding drugs. . . .

Before reviewing the evidence that profiling critics offer, recall the demands that the police face every day, far from anti-police agitators and their journalist acolytes. February 22, 2001, a town-hall meeting at [Police Station] 153 in Harlem between New York mayor Rudolph Giuliani and Harlem residents: a woman sarcastically asks Giuliani if police officers downtown are paid more than uptown officers, "because we don't have any quality of life in Harlem, none whatsoever. Drug dealers are allowed to stand out in front of our houses every day, to practically invade us, and nothing's done about it." Another woman complains that dealers are back on the street the day after being arrested, and notes that "addicts are so bold that we have to get off the sidewalk and go around *them!*" She calls for the declaration of a state of emergency. A man wonders if cop-basher congressman Charles Rangel, present at the meeting, could "endow the police with more power," and suggests that the NYPD [New York Police Department] coordinate with the federal Drug Enforcement Administration, the INS [Immigration and Naturalization Service], and the IRS [Internal Revenue Service] to bring order to the streets. . . .

This is the demand—often angry, sometimes wistful—that urban police forces constantly hear: *get rid of the drugs!* . . .

In New York, the mayhem eventually led to the development of the Giuliani administration's assertive policing that strives, quite successfully, to prevent crime from happening. Outside of New York, the widespread pleas to stop drug violence led the Drug Enforcement Administration to enlist state highway police in their anti-drug efforts. The DEA and the Customs Service had been using intelligence about drug routes and the typical itineraries of couriers to interdict drugs at airports; now the interdiction war would expand to the nation's highways, the major artery of the cocaine trade.

The DEA taught state troopers some common identifying signs of drug couriers: nervousness; conflicting information about origin and destination cities among vehicle occupants; no luggage for a long trip; lots of cash; lack of a driver's license or insurance; the spare tire in the back seat; rental license plates or plates from key source states like Arizona and New Mexico; loose screws or scratches near a vehicle's hollow spaces, which can be converted to hiding places for drugs and guns. The agency also shared intelligence about the types of cars that couriers favored on certain routes, as well as about the ethnic makeup of drug-trafficking organizations. A typical DEA report from the early 1990s noted that "large-scale interstate trafficking networks controlled by Jamaicans, Haitians, and black street gangs dominate the manufacture and distribution of crack.". . . .

Black motorists today almost routinely claim that the only reason they are pulled over for highway stops is their race. Once they are pulled over, they say, they are subject to harassment, including traumatic searches. Some of these tales are undoubtedly true. Without question, there are obnoxious officers out there, and some officers may ignore their training and target minorities. But since the advent of video cameras in patrol cars, installed in the wake of the racial profiling controversy, most charges of police racism, testified to under oath, have been disproved as lies. . . .

Despite the hue and cry, there is nothing illegal about using race as one factor among others in assessing criminal suspiciousness. Nevertheless, the initial decision to pull a car over should be based almost always on seriousness of traffic violation alone—unless, of course, evidence of other law-breaking, such as drug use, is visible. . . .

Soft racial profiling was probably not widespread enough to have influenced traffic-stop rates significantly. Nor will eliminating it quickly change the belief among many blacks that any time they get stopped for a traffic violation, it is because of their race. Nevertheless, state police commanders should eliminate any contribution that soft profiling may make to that perception, unless strong evidence emerges (as it has not so far) that soft profiling has had an extremely high success rate in drug interdiction. Far more is at stake here than the use of race in traffic stops. Specious anti-racial profiling analysis threatens to emasculate policing in areas where drug enforcement is on a far stronger basis.

The most important victory of the anti–racial profiling agitators occurred not on the traffic-stop battlefield, but on the very different terrain of the searches that sometimes follow a stop. And here is where people who care about law enforcement should really start to worry. On April 20, 1999, New Jersey's then–attorney general Peter Verniero issued his "Interim Report of the State Police Review Team Regarding Allegations of Racial Profiling." It was a bombshell, whose repercussions haven't stopped yet.

"The problem of disparate treatment [of blacks] is real, not imagined," the report famously declared. Governor Christine Todd Whitman chimed in: "There is no question that racial profiling exists at some level." The media triumphantly broadcast the findings as conclusive proof of racial profiling not just in the Garden State but nationally. The *New York Times* started regularly referring to New Jersey's "racial bias" on the highways as incontrovertible fact. . . .

Mountains of Ambiguous Statistics

It is not very surprising to learn that the main fruit of the "racial profiling" hysteria has been a decline in the efficiency of police work. In Philadelphia, a federal court order now requires police to fill out both sides of an 8½-by-11 sheet on every citizen contact. Law-enforcement agencies nationwide are engaged in similar statistics-gathering exercises, under pressure from federal lawmakers like U.S. Rep. John Conyers, who has announced that he will introduce a bill to force police agencies to keep detailed information about traffic stops. ("The struggle goes on," declared Rep. Conyers. The struggle that is going on, it sometimes seems, is a struggle to prevent our police forces from accomplishing any useful work at all.)

The mountain of statistics that is being brought forth by all this panic does not, on the evidence so far, seem likely to shed much light on what is happening. The numbers have a way of leading off into infinite regresses of uncertainty. The city of San Jose, Calif., for example, discovered that, yes, the percentage of blacks being stopped was higher than their representation in the city's population. Ah, but patrol cars were computer-assigned to high-crime districts, which are mainly inhabited by minorities. So that over-representation might actually be an under-representation! But then, minorities have fewer cars.

John Derbyshire, "In Defense of Racial Profiling," *National Review*, February 19, 2001.

Yet the report's influential analysis is shoddy beyond belief. Contrary to popular perception, Verniero did not reach any conclusions about racial profiling in stops. His finding of "disparate treatment" is based on the percentage of "consent searches" performed on minorities *after* a stop has occurred. (In a consent search, the motorist agrees to allow the trooper to search his car and person, without a warrant or probable cause.) Between 1994 and 1998, claims the report,

53 percent of consent searches on the southern end of the New Jersey Turnpike involved a black person, 21 percent involved whites, and overall, 77 percent involved minorities. But these figures are meaningless, because Verniero does not include racial information about search requests that were denied, and his report mixes stops, searches, and arrests from different time periods.

But most important: Verniero finds culpable racial imbalance in the search figures without suggesting a proper benchmark. He simply assumes that 53 percent black consent searches is too high. Compared with what? If blacks in fact carry drugs at a higher rate than do whites, then this search rate merely reflects good law enforcement. If the police are now to be accused of racism every time that they go where the crime is, that's the end of public safety.

The hue and cry over the alleged New Jersey search rate makes sense only if we assume that drug trafficking is spread evenly across the entire population and that officers are unable to detect the signs of a courier once they have pulled over a car. There are powerful reasons to reject both these assumptions.

Judging by arrest rates, minorities are vastly overrepresented among drug traffickers. Blacks make up over 60 percent of arrests in New Jersey for drugs and weapons, though they are 13.5 percent of the population. Against such a benchmark, the state police search rates look proportionate.

The attorney general's report dismissed this comparison with an argument that has become *de rigueur* among the anti–racial profiling crowd, even in Congress: the "circularity" argument. Arrest and conviction data for drugs and weapons are virtually meaningless, said Verniero. They tell you nothing about the world and everything about the false stereotypes that guide the police. If the police find more contraband on blacks and Hispanics, that is merely because they are looking harder for it, driven by prejudiced assumptions. If the police were to target whites with as much enforcement zeal, goes this reasoning, they would find comparable levels of criminality. David Harris, a University of Toledo law school professor and the leading expert for the anti-profiling forces, makes this preposterous argument. An enforcement effort directed at 40-year-old white law professors, he assures a Senate subcommittee, would yield noticeable busts. The disproportionate minority arrests then reinforce the initial, racist stereotypes, and the vicious cycle begins all over again—too many minorities arrested, too many whites going free.

The circularity argument is an insult to law enforcement and a prime example of the anti-police advocates' willingness to rewrite reality. Though it is hard to prove a negative—in this case, that there is *not* a large cadre of white drug lords operating in the inner cities—circumstantial evidence rebuts the activists' insinuation. Between 1976 and 1994, 64 percent of the homicide victims in drug turf wars were black, according to a Heritage Foundation analysis of FBI data. Sixty-seven percent of known perpetrators were also black. Likewise, some 60 percent of victims and perpetrators in drug-induced fatal brawls are black. These figures match the roughly 60 percent of drug offenders in state prison who are black. Unless you believe that white traffickers are less violent than black traffickers, the arrest, conviction, and imprisonment rate for blacks on drug charges appears consistent with the level of drug activity in the black population. (And were it true that white dealers *are* less violent, wouldn't we expect police to concentrate their enforcement efforts on the most dangerous parts of the drug trade?)

The notion that there are lots of heavy-duty white dealers sneaking by undetected contradicts the street experience of just about every narcotics cop you will ever talk to—though such anecdotal evidence, of course, would fail to convince the ACLU [American Civil Liberties Union], convinced as it is of the blinding racism that afflicts most officers. "The hard-core sellers are where the hard-core users are—places like 129th Street in Harlem," observes Patrick Harnett, retired chief of the narcotics division for the NYPD. "It's not white kids from Rockland County who are keeping black sellers in business."

The cops go where the deals are. When white club owners, along with Israelis and Russians, still dominated the Ecstasy trade, that's whom the cops were arresting. Recently, however, big shipments have been going to minority neighborhoods; subsequent arrests will reflect crime intelligence, not racism.

There's not a single narcotics officer who won't freely admit that there are cocaine buys going down in the men's bathrooms of Wall Street investment firms—though at a small fraction of the amount found on 129th Street. But that is not where community outrage, such as that Mayor Giuliani heard in Harlem, is directing the police, because they don't produce violence and street intimidation.

Ultimately, the circularity argument rests on a massive denial of reality, one that is remarkably vigorous and widespread. In March 2000, for example, New Jersey senator Robert Torricelli asserted before then-senator John Ashcroft's Judiciary Subcommittee: "Statistically it cannot bear evidence [*sic*] to those who suggest, as our former superintendent of the state police suggested, that certain ethnic or racial groups disproportionately commit crimes. They do not." Needless to say, Torricelli did not provide any statistics. . . .

The bottom line is this: the New Jersey attorney general has branded the state police as racist without a scintilla of analysis for his finding. Yet New Jersey is the wave of the future, for racial profiling data-collection initiatives are sweeping the country. At least 30 states could soon require their state police to collect racial data on all traffic stops and searches, with the stated end of eliminating "racial profiling." Urban forces are under identical pressure. . . .

Urban police chiefs worry about the data-collection mania as much as highway patrol commanders do. Ed Flynn, chief of police for Virginia's Arlington County, explains why. [In 2000], the black community in his jurisdiction was demanding heavier drug enforcement. "We had a series of community meetings. The residents said to us: 'Years ago, you had control over the problem. Now the kids are starting to act out again.' They even asked us: 'Where are your jump-out squads [who observe drug deals from their cars, then jump out and nab the participants]?'" So Flynn and his local commander put together an energetic strategy to break up the drug trade. They instituted aggressive motor-vehicle checks throughout the problem neighborhood. Cracked windshield, too-dark windows, expired tags, driving too fast? You're getting stopped and questioned. "We wanted to increase our presence in the area and make it quite unpleasant for the dealers to operate," Flynn says. The Arlington officers also cracked down on quality-of-life offenses like public urination, and used undercover surveillance to take out the dealers.

By the end of the summer, the department had cleaned up the crime hot spots. Community newsletters thanked the cops for breaking up the dealing. But guess what? Says Flynn: "We had also just generated a lot of data showing 'disproportionate' minority arrests." The irony, in Flynn's view, is acute. "We are responding to heartfelt demands for increased police presence," he says. "But this places police departments in the position of producing data at the community's behest that can be used against them.". . .

However much the racial profilers try to divert attention away from the facts of crime, those facts remain obdurate. Arlington has a 10 percent black population, but robbery victims identify nearly 70 percent of their assailants as black. In 1998, blacks in New York City were 13 times more likely than whites to commit a violent assault, according to victim reports. As long as those numbers remain unchanged, police statistics will also look disproportionate. This is the crime problem that black leaders should be shouting about.

But the politics of racial profiling has taken over everything else. Here again, New Jersey is a model of profiling pandering, and it foreshadows the irrationality that will beset the rest of the country. In February 1999, New Jersey governor Christine Todd Whitman peremptorily fired the head of the state police, Colonel Carl Williams, whose reputation for honesty had earned him the nickname "The Truth." It was the truth that got him fired. The day before his dismissal, Williams had had the temerity to tell a newspaper reporter that minority groups dominate the cocaine and marijuana trade.

Of course, this information had constituted the heart of DEA reports for years. No matter. Stating it publicly violated some collective fairy tale that all groups commit drug crimes at equal rates. . . .

New Jersey will soon monitor the length of traffic stops that individual officers make and correlate it to the race of the motorist. It will also monitor by race the computer checks that individual officers run on license plates, on the theory that racist officers will spend more time bothering innocent black motorists and will improperly target them for background checks. Of course an officer's stop and arrest data will be closely scrutinized for racial patterns as well. And if in fact such investigatory techniques correlate with race because more minorities are breaking the law? Too bad for the cop. He will be red-flagged as a potential racist.

These programs monitoring individual officers are present in all jurisdictions that, like New Jersey, operate under a federal monitor. Along with the new state requirements for racial data collection on a department-wide basis, they will destroy assertive policing, for they penalize investigatory work. The political classes are telling police officers that if they have "too many" enforcement interactions with minorities, it is because they are racists. Officers are responding by cutting back enforcement. Drug arrests dropped 55 percent on the Garden State Parkway in New Jersey in 2000, and 25 percent on the turnpike and parkway combined. When the mayor and the police chief of Minneapolis accused Minneapolis officers of racial profiling, traffic stops dropped 63 percent. Pittsburgh officers, under a federal consent decree monitoring their individual enforcement actions, now report that they are arresting by racial quota. Arrests in Los Angeles, whose police department has been under fire from the Justice Department, dropped 25 percent in the first nine months of 2000, while homicides jumped 25 percent.

The Harlem residents who so angrily demanded more drug busts from Mayor Giuliani last February [2001] didn't care about the race of the criminals who were destroying their neighborhood. They didn't see "black" or "white." They only saw dealers—and they wanted them out. That is precisely the perspective of most police officers as well; their world is divided into "good people" and "bad people," not into this race or that.

If the racial profiling crusade shatters this commonality between law-abiding inner-city residents and the police, it will be just those law-abiding minorities who will pay the heaviest price.

"Adolescents are not small adults, and should not be treated or punished as if they were." , young people

Juvenile Offenders Should Not Be Treated as Adults

Patrick T. McCormick

Patrick T. McCormick is an associate professor of Christian ethics at Gonzaga University in Spokane, Washington. In the following viewpoint he criticizes the growing practice of trying juvenile offenders as if they were adults, incarcerating juvenile offenders with adults, and even putting prisoners to death for crimes they committed as minors. McCormick argues that psychological research—as well as common sense—shows that adolescents think and judge differently than adults, and that punishing them as if they were adults is therefore unfair. Moreover, he warns, doing so may be detrimental to society, since juvenile offenders tried and punished as adults are more likely to offend again.

As you read, consider the following questions:

1. How many juvenile offenders were being held in prisons and adult correctional institutions in 1998, according to the author?
2. How many states does McCormick claim allow persons under the age of eighteen to be tried as adults?
3. In McCormick's view, what are some of the dangers that adolescents in adult jails and prisons face?

Patrick T. McCormick, "Fit to Be Tried?" *American Enterprise*, vol. 186, February 11, 2002, p. 15. Copyright © 2002 by the American Enterprise Institute for Public Policy Research. Reproduced by permission of The American Enterprise, a magazine of Politics, Business, and Culture. On the Web at www.TAEmag.com.

Imagine a 12-year-old boy who has committed a brutal, senseless homicide. Now imagine a 47-year-old legislator who claims this child should be treated as if he were a mature adult. Which of these is behaving like a grown-up?

[In 2001] prosecutors in Florida put two 14-year-olds on trial as adults for homicides committed when the youngsters were 12 and 13 years of age. A Fort Lauderdale jury convicted Lionel Tate of first-degree murder in the 1999 death of 6-year-old Tiffany Eunick, and the judge imposed a mandatory sentence of life without parole. Four months later a West Palm Beach jury found Nathaniel Brazill guilty of second-degree murder and the 14-year-old was sentenced to 28 years in prison without parole for killing his English teacher, Barry Grunow. Meanwhile, a superior court in California has ruled that 15-year-old Charles Andrew Williams should be tried as an adult for the murder of two students in a school shooting [in March 2001].

In these states we would not let a 12- or 13-year-old buy a carton of cigarettes, a six-pack of beer or a ticket to the movie "American Pie 2." They are not mature, competent or responsible enough to drive a car, get a job, move out of the house, marry, serve in the military or vote. They need a note from their parents to go on a class trip to the zoo. But let a 12-year-old do something truly monstrous, and suddenly state and federal lawmakers want to behave as if this child were competent to stand trial as an adult in a capital murder case—as if it made sense to punish this prepubescent adolescent in the same way we would a hardened felon.

A Growing Trend

And Masters Tate, Brazill and Williams are just the tip of the iceberg. Over the past decade legislators in 47 states and the District of Columbia have made it easier to put on trial and punish juveniles as adults. Between 1985 and 1997 the number of minors admitted to state prisons more than doubled, climbing from 3,400 to 7,400. In 1998 U.S. jails housed nearly 7,000 youngsters awaiting trial, and prisons and adult correctional facilities held more than 11,000 juveniles. That same year state and federal prosecutors charged 200,000 young people with criminal offenses.

Children in U.S. prisons or jails are not a new phenomenon. Before 19th-century reformers established America's first juvenile court in Chicago in 1899, children who had reached the age of reason (7) were often tried and sentenced along with adults, serving time in the same prisons and occasionally facing execution. In the period from 1870 to 1890, one out of every 25 convicts in San Quentin and Folsom prisons was between 14 and 17.

But for most of the [twentieth] century, juvenile courts and correction facilities have treated youngsters between 7 and 17 not as criminals but as delinquents, and (in theory at least) focused on rehabilitating the youthful offender rather than punishing the offense. Unlike criminal courts, the proceedings here were not adversarial, but informal and confidential. And juveniles were not convicted or sent to prison, but adjudicated delinquent and put on probation or sent to training schools or reformatories.

Two underlying beliefs have guided the practice of these juvenile courts: first, that children and adolescents are not responsible for their actions in the same way as adults; and second, that they are more open to reform and rehabilitation than their elders. Because of the immaturity and malleability of juveniles, their guilt was weighed differently, and rehabilitation took priority over punishment.

But not all juveniles were kept out of criminal court. Judges in juvenile courts could transfer youths who were nearly 18, habitual offenders or guilty of particularly serious crimes, and down through the years about 1 percent of youthful offenders were sent to adult court by means of these judicial waivers.

But in the early 1990's, legislators in nearly every state responded to concerns about a spike in juvenile violent crime rates and began tinkering with the juvenile justice system, making it easier to put more and younger adolescents on trial as adults and to send them to adult jails and prisons—sometimes for life, occasionally for death. State and federal lawmakers made a number of changes in the juvenile justice system. They expanded judicial waivers, allowing judges to transfer younger and less serious offenders to adult court, and they increased the number of cases in which judges are presumed or mandated to issue waivers. They gave prosecutors new or expanded authority to file charges against minors in criminal court, passed legislation excluding certain offenses from juvenile courts and in some states even lowered the age at which all juveniles must be sent to adult court. They also introduced blended sentences, allowing juvenile offenders to finish the last years or decades of their term in adult prisons. And they demanded mandatory minimum sentences for a variety of juvenile offenses.

As it turns out, the surge in juvenile violent crime rates that began in the late 1980's was already ending as legislators made these changes, and could have been better dealt with by limiting adolescents' access to handguns. These, at least, were the findings of a recent report by the Sentencing Project, a Washington-based research group, titled Prosecuting Juveniles in Adult Court. Still, shaken by stories of "superpredators" and school shootings, lawmakers decided to get tough on juvenile crime and shift the focus from rehabilitating offenders to punishing offenses. As a result, the vast majority of states now allow 14-year-olds to be tried as adults. Fifteen states explicitly permit this practice for children as young as 13, 12 or 10. And more than half the states have one offense for which juveniles of any age can be charged as adults. At the same time, 38 states house juveniles in the general population in adult prisons or jails.

Life Imprisonment and Capital Punishment

Still, our toughness on juveniles is not limited to this new willingness to try and punish more and younger children as adults. America's judicial system can also boast an uncommon and unpopular readiness to sentence juveniles to life, or death. The Convention on the Rights of the Child, an international treaty ratified by every U.N. member except the United States and Somalia, forbids punishing any crime committed by a minor with life imprisonment without parole. But in 1998 California had 14 prisoners serving this sentence for crimes committed when they were 16 or 17. And, of course, Lionel Tate received this punishment for a crime he committed as a 12-year-old.

Meanwhile, as we saw in all the furor last August [2001]

over the Texas inmate Napoleon Beazley, America remains one of a handful of countries that execute juvenile offenders. At 17 Beazley murdered John Luttig, and at 25 he was scheduled to become the 19th person executed in the United States since 1976 for a crime committed as a minor. Sentencing juvenile offenders to death is in clear violation of a number of U.N. conventions and treaties and has been condemned by the American Bar Association, most major religious denominations and just about every human rights group with a Web site. Even China gave up the practice in 1997. Still, the U.S. Supreme Court has upheld the constitutionality of executing people over 16, and 23 states currently allow capital punishment for juveniles. So approximately 80 U.S. prisoners sit on death row waiting to be executed for crimes they committed at 16 or 17, and in the last decade over half of the world's executions of juvenile offenders have been in the United States. More than half of those were carried out in Texas.

From all the media attention given to cases like those of Beazley, Tate, Brazill and Williams, it would be easy to conclude that the vast majority of juveniles being tried as adults are violent offenders, probably murderers. But, in Gershwin's phrase, it ain't necessarily so. In both 1995 and 1996 fewer than half the cases nationwide waived to criminal court involved violence against people. And a study released in October 2000, *Youth Crime/Adult Time*, found that current laws cast too wide a net, sending many juveniles into adult courts and jails for nonviolent offenses. According to the study, nearly 40 percent of the juveniles tried as adults were charged with nonviolent crimes, and many were not convicted or were sent back to juvenile court, which suggests that their cases were neither strong nor serious. "The findings suggest that the adult criminal court is taking on numerous cases that should be prosecuted in the juvenile justice system."

The Differences Between Adolescents and Adults

Ironically enough, legislators and prosecutors are charging and punishing more and more juveniles as adults at the very moment researchers are confirming just how different adolescents are from grown-ups. According to a report by a National Research Council panel, titled *Juvenile Crime, Juvenile Justice,* children and adolescents think, feel and judge differently than adults—often overestimating their grasp of a situation and underestimating the negative consequences of their actions.

Recent brain studies indicate that children and adolescents process emotionally charged information in that part of the brain responsible for instinct and gut reaction, while adults do this work in the more "rational" frontal section. Other research shows that while strong emotions can cloud or distort judgments for both adults and adolescents, teens experience wider and more frequent mood swings. All of this suggests that juveniles lack the cognitive and emotional maturity of adults, are less able to think rationally or clearly when faced with emotionally charged decisions and should be held less culpable for their choices.

Auth. © 1999 by Universal Press Syndicate. Reproduced by permission.

At the same time, studies of juvenile defendants raise questions about their capacity to grasp the adversarial process of criminal court and their competence to stand trial as adults. Youngsters under 15 often misunderstand their legal rights and are more likely to confess in detail to an authority figure. Children find it more difficult to remember or recount events in a consistent or coherent fashion. They often forget names, addresses and the correct sequence of events, making it more difficult for them to assist in their defense and easier for police or prosecutors to discredit their testimony. On the witness stand children often appear unemotional and callous, even though they are deeply frightened or upset. And when faced with plea offers from the prosecution, juveniles have a poor grasp of the strength of the case against them or the long-term consequences of their decision. When Nathaniel Brazill realized he was facing a prison sentence of more than a quarter-century, his response was, "Not too bad"—hardly an indication that he understood what was going on.

And if it is a mistake to put juveniles on trial as adults, it may be a greater one to incarcerate them with grown-ups. Adolescents in adult jails and prisons are more vulnerable to a wide range of dangers. Compared with youngsters in juvenile detention centers, youths housed in adult jails are nearly eight times as likely to commit suicide. They are five times as likely to be sexually assaulted, and twice as likely to be beaten by staff members. And they are 50 percent more likely to be attacked with a weapon. A story in the *Miami Herald* suggests that youngsters in Florida prisons are nearly 21 times as likely to report being assaulted or injured as adolescents in the state's juvenile justice system.

Nor does treating juveniles as adults make our communities or society any safer. About 80 percent of juveniles admitted to prison are released before their 21st birthday, and being jailed with adults does not seem to discourage them from returning to a life of crime. If anything, the opposite may be true. Studies in Florida, Pennsylvania, New York and New Jersey and a good deal of national research indicate that recidivism rates are higher among juveniles who are transferred to adult court than among those who remain in the juvenile system. Adolescents who are tried and punished as adults are more likely to offend again, to do so sooner and more often, and to commit more serious crimes than those kept in juvenile court. States like Florida that prosecute large numbers of juveniles as adults have some of the highest juvenile violent-crime rates. And even deterrence programs like Scared Straight, which sought to deter juvenile offenders by exposing them briefly to prison life and adult convicts, have been an unmitigated disaster and led to increased criminal behavior on the part of adolescents.

Indeed, the evidence suggests that several community-based programs that do not involve imprisonment are both less costly and more effective than trying and punishing adolescents as adults. As the authors of *Juvenile Crime, Juvenile Justice* note, "Research has shown that treating most juvenile offenders within the community does not compromise public safety and may even improve it through reduced recidivism.". . .

More than a century after the first juvenile court was founded in Chicago, we have even more reason to know that adolescents are not small adults, and should not be treated or punished as if they were. Children may gain an elementary grasp of morality at 7, but this is not the only age or stage of reason. Developmental psychology has confirmed what Shakespeare told us long ago, that we go through several stages in our cognitive, affective and moral development, and that between the adult and the infant is the "whining school-boy" or adolescent. If we are to play the part of mature adults (Shakespeare's judge), we will need to know the differences between these stages and act accordingly.

"There is a reason [some] children are handled like dangerous criminals: They are dangerous."

Some Juvenile Offenders Should Be Treated as Adults

Christine Stolba

Christine Stolba is a senior fellow at the Independent Women's Forum, a conservative advocacy organization. In the following viewpoint she defends the practice of trying violent juvenile offenders in adult courts. Stolba traces the rise of juvenile courts in the nineteenth century, explaining that they were intended to help rescue minors from adult prisons and to help rehabilitate juvenile offenders. But in the 1960s, she maintains, two Supreme Court decisions stripped juvenile courts of much of their authority, and in the 1980s rising juvenile murder rates led the public to question their effectiveness. Stolba argues that the movement to try violent juvenile offenders as adults is an understandable result of the failure of juvenile courts. In addition, she maintains that juvenile courts have always sent their most dangerous juvenile criminals to adult courts.

As you read, consider the following questions:

1. In the eighteenth century, according to the author, at what age were children deemed to be fully responsible for their actions?
2. Why did juvenile courts come under attack in the 1950s and 1960s, in Stolba's view?
3. What case of teen murder in England does the author cite as galvanizing support for the movement to try juveniles as adults?

Christine Stolba, "Old Enough to Kill," *Women's Quarterly*, Autumn 2001, p. 11. Copyright © 2001 by the Independent Women's Forum. Reproduced by permission of the Independent Women's Forum, www.iwf.org.

Fourteen-year-old Nathaniel Brazill sat quietly in his starched khaki shirt and neatly knotted black tie. Wreathed in baby fat, wearing a quizzical expression, the Florida teenager was on trial for murder as an adult.

A spate of recent cases involving young killers—among them mop-topped Californian Andy Williams, fifteen, who took a gun to school and killed two classmates, and Lionel Tate, another Florida teen, who pummeled a six-year-old neighbor to death—has renewed debate about the way courts treat juvenile offenders and the effectiveness of our separate juvenile justice system.

Should the courts treat children the same way they treat adults? Are children capable of understanding the full import of their actions and do they deserve a shot at rehabilitation? And is the juvenile justice system capable of dealing with minors who commit truly heinous crimes?

The Rise of Juvenile Courts

Juvenile court is a fairly recent development. An offender who lived in the eighteenth century and was seven or older would, in all likelihood, have been treated as an adult by the courts. At that time, the law considered children under the age of seven as lacking full moral capacity and incapable of giving consent. Once children reached the age of seven, however, the courts didn't hesitate to mete out harsh punishments. According to University of Richmond law professor Robert E. Shepherd, who has studied the history of juvenile justice, before 1900, at least ten children were executed in the U.S. for crimes they committed before they were fourteen.

In the nineteenth century, reformers, concerned about the bad effects on children being imprisoned with adult criminals—the "contamination of incorrigible adults," as one put it—formed organizations such as the Society for the Prevention of Juvenile Delinquency, which in 1825 opened a house of refuge in New York to rehabilitate juvenile offenders. The goal of these facilities, which were privately owned, was to rehabilitate and educate youthful delinquents, on the theory that children and adolescents were more capable of reformation than adults. At the same time, reformers believed that children had less moral capacity than adults and thus shouldn't be held to the same standards of culpability. Delinquent children in these houses of refuge performed day labor, toiling at tasks such as tailoring and silver plating, according to Shepherd.

Groups such as the New York Children's Aid Society; which was established in 1853, carried on similar activities. The society, founded by the Reverend Charles Loring Brace, played a preventive role by targeting at-risk urban youth—usually vagrant and abused children—rather than criminal and delinquent kids. The Aid Society's rescued rascals were shipped off to farms and small towns out west to prevent them from embarking on a life of crime.

By century's end, however, a new breed of reformer began criticizing these private children's homes, particularly as the facilities evolved from small houses of refuge into larger reformatories that resembled adult prisons, losing their rehabilitation role in the process.

In an effort to combat these conditions, reformers turned to state governments. Their first success came in 1899, when the first state juvenile court convened in Chicago. The court was the product of years of activism by Progressive era reformers who believed that the focus of juvenile justice should not be on innocence or guilt, but on education, rehabilitation, and the protection of children, particularly those who found themselves in less-than-ideal family situations. Underpinning the juvenile court was the doctrine of parens patriae—the state as benevolent parent.

Most of the crimes brought before the juvenile judge in the early days were a far cry from the violent murders we see kids committing today. In her memoir, *Twenty Years at Hull House*, early twentieth-century settlement house worker Jane Addams wrote of how she and her fellow Progressives in Chicago had become "distressed by the gangs of very little boys who would sally forth with an enterprising leader" in search of houses to plunder, often using the proceeds from their thefts to "buy cigarettes and beer or even candy, which could be conspicuously consumed in the alleys where they might enjoy the excitement of being seen and suspected by the 'coppers.'"

By 1925, forty-six states had some form of juvenile justice

system that exercised original jurisdiction over criminal offenses involving children under the age of eighteen. Juvenile courts were characterized by less formal hearings, often without lawyers, and greater discretion in determining punishment and treatment. The new juvenile courts usually provided greater privacy protections than regular criminal courts, sealing the records of child offenders. The informality of the court proceedings and the procedural latitude granted the judges was meant to put children at ease; it also, not surprisingly, succeeded in eliciting many confessions from children who became comfortable divulging all to their "friend," the judge.

Juvenile Courts Under Attack

This Progressive era treatment model—"rehabilitation through individualized justice," as reformers called it—continued to hold the support of the juvenile justice community during the thirties and forties. But beginning in the 1950s and reaching full flower in the 1960s, juvenile courts became the object of harsh criticism. From the right came cries that juvenile courts were too soft on crime; from the left came an even more vociferous attack. These critics contended that the courts failed to provide juvenile offenders with basic rights to due process.

Eventually the questions surrounding the effectiveness and scope of the juvenile court system reached the U.S. Supreme Court. Two cases in particular proved seminal: *Kent v. United States* (1966) and *In re Gault* (1967). In the Kent case, the Court ruled that the juvenile defendant, sixteen-year-old Morris Kent, who was accused of rape and robbery, had been denied basic constitutional rights by the juvenile court. In the Gault case, the Court further weakened the principle of parens patriae when it found that the juvenile court in Arizona had violated fifteen-year-old Gerald Gault's Fourteenth Amendment right to due process. Young Gault, accused of making lewd telephone calls to a neighbor, was not provided with legal counsel.

Congress weighed in as well by passing the Juvenile Delinquency Prevention and Control Act of 1968, which recommended that nonviolent, noncriminal juvenile offenders (those arrested for infractions such as truancy) be handled by agencies other than the courts. By the 1970s, according to the Department of Justice, "community-based programs, diversion, and deinstitutionalization" were the hallmarks of juvenile justice policy. Most states also enacted laws providing that juvenile offenders be kept separate from adult offenders while serving their sentences.

Juvenile Murder Offenders, 1980–1997

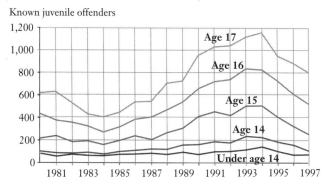

National Center for Juvenile Justice, *Juvenile Offenders and Victims: 1999 National Report*, September 1999.

Although many of the changes were initially viewed as positive, their long-term effects have not been. Author Kay Hymowitz has argued that, in the wake of the *Gault* decision, juvenile courts ended up focusing more on technical legalisms than on their original mission of rehabilitating individual children. "For all its considerable faults," Hymowitz argued in *Ready or Not: Why Treating Children as Small Adults Endangers Their Future—and Ours*, "the old juvenile court was designed so that all adults—parents, teachers, judges—were in a conspiracy to teach adolescents their moral and civic responsibilities. Gault forced that conspiracy to disband."

The conspiracy of the well-meaning adult world is now near extinction. Jane Addams recalled her success in convincing "the firms manufacturing moving picture films not only [to] submit their films to a volunteer inspection committee," but also to encourage the "five-cent theaters" to sponsor "entertaining" and "instructive" lectures on "the subject of public health and morals." Nowadays, as Tipper Gore's music lyrics crusade and New York City mayor Rudolph Giuliani's "decency" commission revealed, adults can't even agree on standards of public morality.

Juvenile courts faced another challenge in the late 1980s and early 1990s: rising juvenile murder rates that led to greater public concern over the effectiveness of the juvenile courts.

The Movement to Try Juveniles as Adults

The serious nature of some juvenile crimes also led to a partial reversal of what had been achieved by the Progressive reformers. There was a movement to "waive" certain youths back to adult court. By the 1990s, the movement to try juveniles who committed particularly repugnant crimes as adults had gained momentum. According to the Department of Justice, between 1992 and 1997, all but three states amended their laws to make it easier to try juvenile offenders in regular criminal court, to apply adult sentencing requirements to juveniles, and to remove some of the confidentiality provisions of the juvenile court system.

After the sentencing of Nathaniel Brazill (he was convicted of second-degree murder), the nonprofit organization Sentencing Project, which opposes trying children as adults, asked, "What does it say about the U.S. that we are ready to give up on some of our children and use the tragic events which overtake a few of them as a basis for denying them the opportunity to mature and grow into responsible adults, unhampered by a criminal record and the trauma of prison life?" *Washington Post* columnist Richard Cohen tried to gin up sympathy for Brazill in a column recounting his own childish pranks. His goal was "to remind us all that kids are kids and to suggest that even the worst of them—even the ones who commit murder—are still kids."

Indeed, many juvenile advocates argue that teen killers often don't understand the magnitude or consequences of their crimes. A thirteen-year-old on trial [in 2001] for the brutal murder (committed with three other teens) of sixty-four-year-old Jerry Heimann in Everett, Washington, was described by one reporter as "wide-eyed and a little bewildered" during court proceedings.

But sympathy has proven difficult to sustain in an era when often unrepentant children commit grisly murders. Public outrage recently reached a fever pitch in England, when two eighteen-year-olds—who had kidnapped and brutally murdered a toddler when they were ten years old—were released on parole. Like the infamous case of English teen killer Mary Bell, who in 1968 was convicted of murdering two younger children when she was eleven years old, the two parolees were given new identities and forbidden to return to their hometown.

National data on the number of juvenile cases tried in adult criminal court in the U.S. do not exist, but the Department of Justice reports that the state of Florida grants approximately 5,000 such transfers annually, for example. But there is a reason these children are handled like dangerous criminals: They are dangerous. The Bureau of Justice Statistics data on juvenile offenders reveal that of the approximately 7,000 juveniles serving time in adult prisons, more than half of them are doing so for violent crimes. And these are not twelve-year-old babes in the woods—76 percent of them are seventeen or eighteen years old.

It is also worth recalling that the juvenile justice system has always used the regular criminal courts as a safety valve for the most violent and recalcitrant juvenile offenders. Sanford Fox, who has written about the early juvenile courts, notes that adult courts were used "as a sentencing option in children's cases, both before and after the advent of juvenile court." Even the original juvenile court in Chicago remanded thirty-seven boys to the adult criminal court in its first year of operation.

Balance Optimism with Reality

Contemporary society, with its victim culture, its eager embrace of therapy, and its overly optimistic belief in the powers of social engineering, finds distasteful the idea that some people—and especially children—choose not to change. To be sure, many juvenile offenders are the products of very troubled and abusive environments, and the state still has a responsibility to rescue such children—as the Progressives urged nearly a century ago.

But in assessing the current state of juvenile justice it is also useful to remember the comments of the attorney for the recently paroled Robert Thompson, one of the British boys who murdered the toddler. Writing in London's *Sunday Times*, he admitted that Thompson was "the only child I have ever met who frightened me."

Periodical Bibliography

The following articles have been selected to supplement the diverse views presented in this chapter.

Sasha Abramsky	"Hard-Time Kids," *American Prospect*, August 27, 2001.
Norm R. Allen	"Reforming the Incarceration Nation," *Free Inquiry*, Summer 2001.
Gene Callahan and William Anderson	"The Roots of Racial Profiling," *Reason*, August/September 2001.
Theodore Dalrymple	"Why Prison Works," *New Statesman*, May 7, 2001.
John Derbyshire	"In Defense of Racial Profiling," *National Review*, February 19, 2001.
Gregg Easterbrook	"Run on Sentencing: How the Affluent Got an Exemption in the War on Crime," *New Republic*, April 26, 1999.
Katherine Kersten	"Race to Conclusions: What the Activists Don't Tell You About Racial Profiling," *Weekly Standard*, August 20, 2001.
Jennifer Roback Morse	"Parents or Prisons," *Policy Review*, August/September 2003.
Newsweek	"Death at a Very Early Age," August 28, 2000.
Ron Powers	"The Apocalypse of Adolescence," *Atlantic Monthly*, March 2002.
Eyal Press and Jennifer Washburn	"The At-Risk-Youth Industry," *Atlantic Monthly*, December 2002.
Paul Ruffins	"Fighting to Be Heard: Black Criminologists Seek Proper Context to Explain Racism's Influence on Black Crime," *Black Issues in Higher Education*, January 17, 2002.
J. Steven Smith	"Adult Prisons: No Place for Kids," *USA Today*, July 2002.
Laurence Steinberg	"Should Juvenile Offenders Be Tried as Adults?" *USA Today*, January 2001.
Steven M. Teles and Mark Kleiman	"Escape from America's Prison Policy," *American Prospect*, September 11, 2000.
Time	"What's Race Got to Do with It?" July 30, 2001.

CHAPTER 4

How Can Crime Be Reduced?

Chapter Preface

Police are the members of the criminal justice system who are most immediately involved in reducing crime. In 1999 there were an estimated 13,524 local police departments in the United States, employing about 436,000 full-time sworn officers. The strategies that police employ in fighting crime vary from city to city and even from department to department. Since the early 1990s, however, community policing has emerged as one of the most popular concepts in crime control.

In broad terms, "community policing" simply refers to the practice of police working with the community to reduce crime. The National Institute of Justice report *Preventing Crime: What Works, What Doesn't, What's Promising* highlights several common characteristics of community policing initiatives. The first is neighborhood watch programs, in which neighbors volunteer to monitor streets for criminal activity. The second is intelligence sharing: Through increased bike and foot patrols, community meetings, and other methods, police work to increase contact with members of the community. Through these contacts, police can solicit the community's help in gaining information and also disseminate information about criminal activity. Finally, community policing is designed to help police gain the public's trust, confidence, and respect.

Community policing is on the rise. According to the U.S. Bureau of Justice Statistics (BJS), the percentage of local police officers nationwide who were designated community policing officers surged from 4 percent to 21 percent between 1997 and 1999. BJS reports that as of June 30, 1999, 69 percent of local police departments had met with community groups within the past year, and 40 percent of all departments had formed a problem-solving partnership within the past three years.

Community policing is still evolving, as police departments and communities experiment together with different crime-prevention programs. The viewpoints in the following chapter examine various approaches to controlling crime.

*"The remarkable thing about the death
penalty is why anyone would think it
doesn't deter murder."*

The Death Penalty Deters Murder

William Tucker

William Tucker is a New York–based freelance writer and
the author of *Excluded Americans: Homelessness and Housing
Policy*. In the following viewpoint Tucker argues that the
death penalty is an effective deterrent against murder. He
maintains that the rise in murder rates from the mid-1960s
to the mid-1970s is due in part to states' limited use of the
death penalty during this period, and that the decline in
murder rates since 1993 is partly due to a rise in the use of
capital punishment. Without the death penalty, Tucker argues, criminals are more likely to murder the witnesses to
their crimes, but the fear of capital punishment causes them
to think twice.

As you read, consider the following questions:

1. During what year did all states temporarily cease
   executions?
2. During what period did the murder rate reach its lowest
   level in history, according to Tucker?
3. What category of murder does the author say accounts
   for almost the entire increase in murder from 1966 to
   the mid-1990s?

William Tucker, "The Case for Retaining Capital Punishment/Deterring
Homicides with the Death Penalty," *Human Events*, vol. 59, April 7, 2003, p. 18.
Copyright © 2003 by *Human Events*. Reproduced by permission.

The remarkable thing about the death penalty is why anyone would think it doesn't deter murder. No one wants to die. Why wouldn't the fear of death make people think twice?

Liberals spend a great deal of time running around this point. The best they can come up with is that murderers are stupid. They don't think. They don't plan. They act on impulse. Murders are "crimes of passion." Executing people is only a "barbaric ritual" that does no good.

Once upon a time there were some grounds for this argument. By the early 1960s, almost 90% of murders were "acquaintance" crimes involving friends or relatives. The most common scenario was an argument that escalated into deadly violence. True, it might involve a romantic rivalry or two casually acquainted people arguing over a card game. But these were "crimes of passion," liberals said. They couldn't be deterred.

And so, beginning with the U.S. Supreme Court's "incorporation" of the 4th and 5th Amendments into state criminal proceedings in the early 1960s and ending with the outright overturn of all state death penalties in 1972, executions ground to a halt.

The results can be seen in the accompanying graph. The murder rate had peaked in 1933 during Prohibition. Violence and executions peaked two years later at 200—about four every week. As gang violence subsided, murders and executions followed each other down at a steady pace until the late 1950s and early 1960s when the murder rate reached its lowest level in history.

Then the upswing started. Executions dropped precipitously after 1962 when the Supreme Court started intervening on the basis of *Mapp v Ohio* (1961), *Gideon v Wainwright* (1963) and *Miranda v Arizona* (1966). After 1966, the murder rate soared to unprecedented heights, peaking in 1974, 1980, and again in 1991 before finally dropping again precipitously—when executions were resumed.

What caused this upsurge? There is a fairly simple explanation. Liberals were probably right in arguing in the early 1960s that capital punishment could not deter the 90% of murders that occurred among relatives and acquaintances. What they did not perceive is the murders that were being deterred. These were the "stranger" or "felony" murders that have since come to dominate the murder statistics.

From the criminal's point of view, the logic is fairly simple. When you are committing a felony—either a rape or robbery—there is a certain calculated advantage in murdering your victim. The victim, after all, is also the principal witness to the crime. He or she is the person most likely to put you in jail, by screaming or calling for others, by going to the police immediately after you leave, by identifying you, by testifying against you in court. Murdering the victim "leaves no witnesses."

Executions vs. Murder Rate, 1930–2000

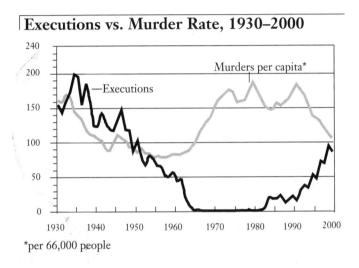

*per 66,000 people

William Tucker, "The Case for Retaining Capital Punishment/Deterring Homicides with the Death Penalty," *Human Events*, April 7, 2003.

Sometimes this is premeditated. Particularly cold, heartless killers will enter a situation knowing they must kill their victims. John Taylor, now under death sentence in New York for the "Wendy's Massacre," was a former employee who gained entrance to the store to commit an after-hours robbery only because his victims knew him and let him in. Taylor and an accomplice then lined them up and shot them. He went into the store knowing he would have to kill each of his victims to avoid identification.

But far more often the killer is an amateur who doesn't realize until the robbery has begun that the victim has "had a good look at him" and must be eliminated.

There is no way to contravene this logic of murder except through the death penalty. No amount of pleading or cajoling—no promises that "I won't tell"—will ever convince a robber or rapist that there isn't an advantage to escalating the crime to murder. The only plausible deterrent is a qualitatively different punishment. If the punishment for robbery is a few years in jail and the punishment for murder is a few more years after that, there is very little if any deterrence. But if the punishment for robbery is jail time and the punishment for murder is death, there is reason to think twice.

The need to draw a bright line between a felony and felony murder was what inspired Enlightenment reformers to argue against capital punishment for crimes less than murder. In *The Spirit of the Laws* (1750), [Baron de] Montesquieu wrote:

"In China, those who add robbery to murder are cut in pieces: but not so the others; to this difference it is owing that though they rob in that country they never murder. In Russia, where the punishment for robbery and murder are the same, they always murder. The dead, they say, tell no tales."

But eliminating the death penalty creates the exact same dilemma. Without any qualitative differential, there is no disincentive to murder the victim of the crime.

Almost the entire increase in murder from 1966 to the mid-1990s was an increase in felony or "stranger" murders—murders committed during the course of another crime. Only when executions resumed in the 1990s did the murder rate drop precipitously to its 1960s level. About 300,000 Americans died unnecessarily in the interim.

A few years ago a New Jersey housewife was kidnapped at a shopping mall by a teenage carjacker. The youth was obviously an amateur and could think of nothing to do but drive the woman around for a few hours. In the process, though, it became obvious that he intended to kill her. The woman spent the better part of an hour pleading for her life. She also had a pocket tape-recorder, which she activated. Over and over she pleads, "Is it worth my life for you to have a car?" The logic did not work. He killed her anyway.

But what if the woman had been able to argue, "Is it worth your life?" Would that have made a difference?

"The death penalty does not lower homicide rates."

The Death Penalty Does Not Deter Murder

Nat Hentoff

Nat Hentoff is a columnist for the *Village Voice* and the author of numerous books on civil liberties, including *The First Freedom: The Tumultuous History of Free Speech in America*. In the following viewpoint Hentoff rejects the claim that the death penalty deters murder. He cites statistics showing that the murder rate in states with the death penalty is higher than the murder rate in states without capital punishment. Moreover, he argues that the death penalty is often applied in cases where the defendant has poor legal defense, and many accused murderers are wrongly convicted. The mistakes and lack of fairness with which the death penalty is applied, he argues, harm the criminal justice system more than the unproven "deterrent effect" helps society.

As you read, consider the following questions:

1. What percentage of American criminologists questioned in the survey that Hentoff cites said that the death penalty does not deter murder?
2. What was the average per capita murder rate in 1998 in states with the death penalty and in states without it, according to the statistics cited in the viewpoint?
3. How have some men on death row been proven innocent and released, according to the author?

Nat Hentoff, "Is Capital Punishment a Deterrent?" *San Diego Union-Tribune*, November 27, 2000, p. B-7. Copyright © 2000 by Nat Hentoff. Reproduced by permission.

Not all opponents of capital punishment speak with one voice. Some, like Justice Harry Blackmun, who supported the death penalty during most of his term on the U.S. Supreme Court, finally decided he would "no longer tinker with the machinery of death" because the ultimate punishment was so randomly applied. That is, some of those on death row had not received due process—basic fairness—in their trials, or in their appeals.

Others, such as the late Catholic cardinals Joseph Bernardin and John Cardinal O'Connor, were against capital punishment because they believed that to be pro-life, one must adhere to a consistent ethic of life—being against abortion, euthanasia and capital punishment.

On the other hand, supporters of the death penalty often agree with George W. Bush and Al Gore. During their third presidential debate, both candidates were asked why they were for the death penalty. Both answered immediately: "It's a deterrence." Without capital punishment, homicides would increase.

Neither Bush nor Gore gave any factual evidence to support their position. They couldn't, because the great weight of evidence is against them.

In 1996, the *Journal of Criminal Law and Criminology* reported that a survey of 70 leading American criminologists found that over 80 percent of them said that the death penalty does not lower homicide rates.

More definitively, on September 22 of [2000], an extensively researched *New York Times* survey revealed that the 12 states without a death penalty have homicide rates below the national average.

As Richard Dieter, executive director of the Death Penalty Information Center, points out, "The average murder rate per 100,000 population in 1998 among states with the death penalty was 6.2. However, the average murder rate among states without the death penalty was only 3.2. A look at neighboring death penalty and non-death-penalty states shows similar trends."

Furthermore, with regard to the uneven fairness of the trials, I have reported on death penalty cases for some 40 years, and it is an undeniable fact that since most of those on death

Too Rare to Be Effective, Too Fraught with Error to Be More Commonplace

The commonest, and most common-sensical, argument for the death penalty is that it deters murder. But numerous studies have failed to establish that execution deters better than a long prison term. Not only has the United States the highest murder rate in the industrialised world, but murder rates there are highest in southern states, where most executions occur. Many subtler studies have analysed murder rates in neighbouring states with and without the death penalty, before and after high-profile executions or before and after the death penalty's abolition or reintroduction. None has found good evidence for deterrence.

In certain ways this is not so surprising. Consider the statistics for the ten years to 1993. About 22,000 criminal homicides were recorded annually in the United States during these years. Of these, only 2,000–4,000 cases were egregious enough to qualify for the death penalty and, on average, 250 actually resulted in a death sentence. And, during these years, only 22 people, on average, were executed annually. So the chances of a killer being caught, prosecuted, convicted and then executed during this period were about one in a thousand. Given these odds, and the vagaries of the criminal justice system, a killer has to be very unlucky indeed to end up being executed.

The number of executions has increased since 1994 to 68 [in 1998] . . . but that does not shorten the odds by much and hardly alters the argument. Moreover, by law the death penalty is supposed to be reserved for perpetrators of the worst sorts of murder, criminals who have killed repeatedly or committed appallingly violent crimes. But these are the people least likely to be rational enough to calculate the consequences of their acts, or to be deterred by the prospect of execution. For the death penalty to be an effective deterrent, America would probably have to execute hundreds, even thousands, every year, not a few dozen. The probability that many more innocent people would also be executed would have to be weighed against the benefits of deterrence. A minority of death-penalty supporters might not mind. But could the majority of Americans stomach it?

Economist, "The Cruel and Ever More Unusual Punishment," May 15, 1999.

---

row cannot afford experienced lawyers, many of those cases are handled by inexperienced court-appointed attorneys, some with little or no previous experience in capital cases.

As reporter Richard Perez-Pena noted in the *New York*

Times (Feb. 12, 2000): "There are states like Texas, Alabama and Georgia, where the death penalty is frequently imposed, and there is no public defender system at all. Instead, judges appoint lawyers for poor defendants and set their compensation, often at low rates." Often very low rates, with minimal funds for investigators and forensic experts.

I interviewed the warden of a prison in Mississippi that had a number of prisoners on death row. I asked him whether it was true that three of them had no lawyers at all after their state appeals were lost. Their only chance to live was if a federal judge were to grant them a writ of habeas corpus so that their trials and sentences could be reviewed in a federal court.

The warden told me my information was accurate.

"Then what recourse do they have, since they have no lawyers?" I asked.

"Well," said the warden, "we have a prison library. There are law books there. They can figure out a way to try to get a writ of habeas corpus."

I asked him how much education those three prisoners had. He paused. "Well," he said, "they didn't have much schooling. But the law books are there."

In the *National Journal* (Feb. 12, 2000), Stuart Taylor—former Supreme Court reporter for the *New York Times* and currently a writer for *Legal Times*—quotes Gerald Kogan, a former chief justice of Florida who has also been a prosecutor and trial judge. Says Kogan:

"There are several cases where I had grave doubts as to the guilt of a particular person" who was put to death.

Increasingly, men on death row—some with execution only days and sometimes hours away—are proved innocent and released because of DNA or the work of volunteer independent investigators.

With not many exceptions, the lawyers who lost the cases of these defendants were incompetent. And that's why Illinois Governor George Ryan, who ran George W. Bush's presidential campaign in that state, has said: "Until I can be sure with moral certainty that no innocent man or woman is facing a lethal injection, no one will meet that fate."

But George W. Bush and Al Gore automatically support this random method of execution because it "deters."

"[Crime] must be viewed as antisocial behavior that can be suppressed if people are held accountable for their acts."

Crime Policies Should Emphasize Strict Policing and Strong Punishment

Karl Zinsmeister

Karl Zinsmeister is editor-in-chief of *American Enterprise* magazine, a publication of the American Enterprise Institute, a conservative research and advocacy organization. In the following viewpoint Zinsmeister argues that "tough-on-crime" policies, including increased policing and longer prison sentences, are responsible for decreasing crime rates. In Zinsmeister's opinion, crime is a matter of individuals committing immoral acts rather than a natural by-product of urban poverty. Zinsmeister believes that the threat of arrest and imprisonment is the most effective means of deterring crime, but he warns that the breakdown of families and liberal activists' criticisms of police are undermining the progress that the United States has made in the fight against crime.

As you read, consider the following questions:

1. When did public attitudes toward law-breaking, personal responsibility, and punishment take a "U-turn," in Zinsmeister's view?
2. What types of misdemeanor laws are enforced in Florida to help keep order, according to the author?
3. What two cities does Zinsmeister identify to show that crime may once again be on the rise?

Karl Zinsmeister, "Crime Is Down, but Far from Out," *American Enterprise*, vol. 12, June 2001, p. 4. Copyright © 2001 by the American Enterprise Institute for Public Policy Research. Reproduced by permission of The American Enterprise, a magazine of Politics, Business, and Culture. On the Web at www.TAEmag.com.

Those of you who had reason to pass through New York City in the dark, going-to-hell-in-a-handbasket days of the late 1970s and early '80s: Remember the signs city residents used to post in their cars when they parked on the street? They read "No Radio." And sure enough, if you peered in at the dashboard you'd see a gaping hole instead of buttons and dials.

Accommodating Criminality

This represented a very frank declaration—good liberals pre-emptively telling thieves, "I surrender." New Yorkers were basically conceding the streets to the pirates, and were advertising that their radios (and all other items of even minor value) had already been stripped out of their private vehicles—either by earlier robbers, or by fully intimidated owners who'd decided to ride in silence rather than risk having their windows bashed in by one of the criminals then vacuuming the streets of anything they could lay their utterly unrestrained hands on.

The implication was that crime is normal, just something you plan for and rationally work around, like rainshowers. The uglier, hidden invitation of the "No Radio" sign was for the thugs to find someone else—someone a little less jadedly savvy—for their next payday. Maybe a tourist from Kansas. ("Try next car" as the vintage cartoon . . . jokes blackly.) What a thoughtful compromise with the criminal class!

Accommodation of criminality of this sort was rampant in Manhattan and many other liberal precincts across America from the 1960s onward. The subways were owned by the graffiti gangsters. Dope peddlers were treated as somewhere between harmless funlovers and chic moral revolutionaries. Stick-up artists and smash-and-grabbers were said not to know better blame racism/stingy government checks/inadequate day care/whatever. Intellectuals like Norman Mailer excused even murder as a courageous political statement of downtrodden folk.

Of course, during that same era there were plenty of other American neighborhoods where the signs in vehicle windows read "This Truck Protected by Smith and Wesson" instead of "No Radio." But among elites, there was a definite trend toward capitulation and tolerance of criminality in post-1960s America.

The end result is captured well in this little vignette by William Bratton, who oversaw the police clean-up of New York starting in 1990. He describes his entry into Gotham from the airport as he arrived for his job interview:

> It looked like something out of a futuristic movie . . . graffiti on every highway wall . . . burned out cars, litter everywhere. Welcome to New York. Then when you reach the first stop light you see the official greeter for the city, [a panhandler in] dirty clothes with a [windshield] squeegee. . . . Then there were the subways. . . . I can remember going through the first turnstile array and watching people leap over turnstiles, crawl under them, anything but pay the fare. Every platform had a cardboard city on either end of it where the homeless had taken up residence. This was a city that had really lost control of itself.

Getting Tough on Crime

Well, I've got news for you: Those soft-on-crime practices, born of the national nervous breakdown we suffered during the Age of Aquarius, are definitely now passe. Public attitudes toward law-breaking, punishment, and personal responsibility took a U-turn toward toughness starting in the 1980s. Support for street crackdowns, for the death penalty, for trying violent juveniles in adult courts, for strict treatment of drug criminals, have all come roaring back from their Flower Power lows. After a multi-decade decline, the punishment that a criminal could expect for a given crime began to rise again in the 1980s. Spending on police tripled. Prison capacity was quadrupled.

And even after all this tightening, 70 percent of Americans still believe our criminal justice system is "not tough enough." (This from the Gallup poll, September 2000.) Goodbye to the idea that there are no bad boys, just bad societies.

Florida is a great place to examine the way liberal platitudes about crime have evaporated. For one thing, the state was damaged more than most by the post-60s crime boom. Some of the Florida neighborhoods where we rode on night police patrols while researching this issue—like Liberty City and Little Haiti in Miami—racked up the highest official crime rates ever recorded in America just a few years ago. And the metro area we spent most of our time in—the Gulf Coast twin cities of Fort Myers and Cape Coral—proved a perfect laboratory for understanding how crime is mutating into new forms.

Cape Coral is a sprawling bedroom community just across the river from Fort Myers. Demographically, it is classic sunbelt suburbia—almost all single-family homes, overwhelmingly white, uniformly mid-income—and we spent lots of time there in order to document the troubling creep of juvenile problems into America's middle class (more on that later). Compared to the Cape, Fort Myers has more of an inner-city profile. It's a typical urbanized municipality, with a downtown, public housing, racial issues, lots of drugs. It has a crime rate four times the national average. (Most Florida cities are way above the national average, which is why we went there.)

All across southern Florida, we quizzed police officers, prison inmates and guards, court officials, and social workers. We asked them what has changed to reduce overall crime rates in America. Their answer: Everything.

Disorders that used to be ignored or fatalistically accepted are once again being cracked down upon. One table of cops we interviewed ticked off a number of examples: "We now enforce open container laws to stop public drinking." "Loitering, panhandling, and other statutes that people had completely forgotten are being revived." "When we have an apartment building or business that becomes a drug or prostitution nest, we go to Nuisance Abatement Boards and they help us shut them down. These boards used to be real unsympathetic, and gave us lots of ACLU-type excuses. But now they work with us."

The deepest source of today's sharpened attack on crime is new public attitudes and demands. As one detective told us, "It's fashionable today to say that 'community-oriented policing' is the best route to safe streets. Myself. I'd turn that around and say 'policing-oriented communities' are the key. The fact is, a police department's approach to crime directly reflects local standards—what the residents as a whole have decided they will or will not tolerate. In a place with little patience for criminal activity, the policing will be much more active, and there will be a lot less mayhem throughout the city."

The detective continued: "An example of how different community philosophies play out would be our local policy

The Broken Windows Theory

Police leaders, criminologists, and local politicians huddled in the late 80s to try to figure out what they could do against a frighteningly fast-rising national crime problem, which was driving even middle-class blacks to the suburbs and turning once-prosperous downtowns into dead zones. They seized upon the idea that the best place for policemen to be was not in their cruisers, hiding behind windshields and tough-guy sunglasses, but out talking to their people—the people they were assigned to protect—reminding them that the police didn't have to function as a garrison.

This new paradigm, community policing, depended in part on technological advances, which allowed departments to map emerging crime patterns and high-crime areas and shift officers accordingly. But a crucial component of this policy was what came to be known as the "broken windows" theory of crime, whose most prominent proponent was the neoconservative political scientist James Q. Wilson. In ghettos, Wilson argued, the persistent presence of quality-of-life problems like vandalism, abandoned cars, and graffiti had profound psychological effects: It showed residents that the police had lost control of the streets to drug dealers and criminals, shuttering economic activity, signalling to criminals that it was open season on the neighborhood, and keeping residents from calling police when they saw crimes unfolding. Wilson said police should develop a more expansive set of goals, and not be content with simply busting murderers and drug dealers. By vigorously prosecuting small-change crimes like vandalism and graffiti, and by performing social-service functions like helping to get collapsing buildings condemned, cops could give law-abiding residents a sense of neighborhood ownership. By pursuing and jailing criminals for small crimes, the police reduced the number of thugs out on the street likely to commit more violent acts. And when cops won back the streets, residents became less scared about ratting on neighborhood bad guys, which meant the bad guys got arrested more frequently. Wilson's idea turned out, during the late 1990s, to be astoundingly correct.

Benjamin Wallace-Wells, "Bush's War on Cops," *Washington Monthly*, September 2003.

on pursuing stolen cars. In our town, we'll chase car thieves to the ground. We'll dog bite you and drag you to jail. As a result, we suffer fewer than 200 car thefts per year. Meanwhile in the jurisdiction next door, which has a lot less population but refuses to pursue, they have five times as many. A direct result of a policy of giving up."

Officer Olga Rome, a black policewoman we interviewed in Miami, noted that "you know, the new 'community policing'—the grassroots attack on crime that has taken over in the '90s with so many good effects—it really isn't new at all. It's very old. We're basically just going back to more traditional approaches to stopping problems."

She's right. At the moment I'm reading to my youngest child a history of a boy who grew up in Boston around the turn of the century, a time when that city was home to many poor, ignorant, unassimilated, and very rough-mannered families. The streets and schools were often rowdy places. But there was precious little tolerance for crime. Our biography describes how the local foot patrol officer, "Cop Watson" would visit individual homes—warning boys against certain kinds of behaviors, informing parents of juveniles who had gotten their names written down in the "Bad Boy Book" that was stored in the stationhouse (three strikes and the kid was in serious trouble), and otherwise keeping a lid on problems. This kind of stern, moralistic community oversight is why cities full of uneducated, materially deprived people jammed into tenements nonetheless enjoyed comparatively low rates of crime and public disorder.

The key is to treat crime as a preventable, curable, moral breakdown. Crime isn't something natural, something to wave away with a litany of excuses. It must be viewed as antisocial behavior that can be suppressed if people are held accountable for their acts. Officer Rome suggests that having painfully rediscovered this, we're not likely to forget it again. "This time, it's here to stay" she asserts.

Worrisome Trends

Let us hope that the bad old days of accommodating crime truly are permanently behind us. Because two societal trends hint we're going to need plenty of sturdy cops, tough judges, and long-memoried citizens in the years ahead if the progress we've made recently against disorder is going to continue.

Problem trend number one is family decay. The explosion of illegitimacy, divorce, and fatherlessness that ripped particularly through underclass America starting in the 1960s has finally leveled off in those neighborhoods. Inner-city family life hasn't gotten dramatically better, but statistically, black illegitimacy, teen births, and abortion are all down a little. Unfortunately, the family breakdown virus has meantime spread to fresh fields, and is now doing its dirty-work with a vengeance in Middle America. Twenty-six percent of all white births are now to unmarried mothers. That plus the fact that a million children see their parents divorce every year means a vast portion of even middle-class American youngsters now grow up separated from either their dad or mom. That is not good for the crime rate, as even prison inmates will tell you.

Our new suburban delinquency problem is illustrated perfectly in Cape Coral's malls and palm-treed cul-de-sacs. To get a handle on discipline problems, the local elementary schools are now starting to put cops in their hallways. We accompanied police officers on a number of haunting runaway or domestic violence calls. On one, we pulled up to a pristinely manicured new house, where the door was answered by the mother, an attractive nurse supervisor with two children. The interior was gleaming in white tile, new kitchen appliances, and blond furniture. The son, a sandy-haired boy of perhaps 13, was well spoken and crisply dressed in Old Navy khaki, though multiply pierced and accessoried in the local "thug life" fashion (some area teenagers refer to themselves as "wiggers" as in "white niggers").

The mother cooly explained that her 14-year-old daughter "Andrea" has a history of running away, and had skipped school that day, reportedly been picked up by a friend, and was apparently off partying now (near midnight on a school night). As the officer took her missing person report, the mother spelled out Andrea's byzantine criminal record—arrests for shoplifting, stealing a car, battery (beating up her mother). After a radio call, the officer asked her whether she was aware her daughter was on juvenile probation at that time, and should have been kept at home except for schooling. "I'm always at work," she answered, unflustered. "Her father and I are separated. I gave her a pager, and a cell phone, and that's how we keep in touch."

I received several follow-up reports on Andrea. About ten days after my visit to her home, one of her friends convinced her own divorced mother (who knows Andrea's history) to let her sleep over at Andrea's house. Of course, they snuck out for a night of cruising and drug parties. The evening ended with a police report from the mother of Andrea's friend complaining that her daughter had been raped. After enough Ecstacy, cocaine, and pot that she stopped remembering things, the girl was pressured by a white male she had just met until he got his way with her.

A couple months later, Andrea was brought home by sheriffs deputies after being caught in a stolen car with some of the boys she indulges in crime, sex, and drug use with. After arguing with her mother she went into her room and wrote all over the walls with a black marker "my mother is a whore/bitch/c—t, etc." The police eventually took her to a detention center for runaways, which she promptly ran away from, turning up back at home, sneaking along another runaway.

These kinds of stories are no longer rare among middle-class, superficially functional families. In fact, we found serious teenage behavior problems to be actually rather common in households where there is divorce, parents shacking up with new mates, careerism and endless working hours, a lack of deep community roots (a special plague in new sun-belt developments), or substitution of money and material provisions for parental time and guidance. And these things occur even in neighborhoods with lots of fancy cars in the driveways and nice college-educated grown-ups nominally in charge inside the home.

The second trend which might have the power to unravel Officer Rome's prediction that today's progress against crime is here to stay concerns politics. Much sterner public attitudes, and much steelier public administrators (for instance, William Bratton and Rudy Giuliani in New York City) were an important part of our recent crime rollback. But the 1980s and '90s crop of tough reformist mayors like

Giuliani and Richard Riordan in Los Angeles are now about to be replaced by voters, in both cases apparently by liberal throwbacks. When the pressure from City Hall to stop crime eases up (very possibly even reverses, on "progressive" or "civil rights" grounds) control of our urban streets could quickly revert to the people who brought you spray-painted subways and in-your-face panhandling.

Even before these critical political transitions, the consensus against crime that got us on today's downward path has begun to be eroded—by several years of activist hammering on police, politicians, and public opinion. Endless drum-beating about police brutality has undermined both citizen support for cops and cops' willingness to take risks to make streets safer. Renewed propagandizing against capital punishment has recently edged public opinion in a softer direction on this and other crime questions.

The effects are already showing up in statistics. After tumbling for most of a decade, crime edged up in [2000] in places like Los Angeles (where the police have been eviscerated after a corruption scandal) and New York (where movie stars and rabblerousers spent much of 2000 picketing police stations under the instigation of Al Sharpton). Violent crime was up more than 7 percent in L.A. in [2001], with homicides jumping 28 percent. The kinder and gentler NYPD, meanwhile, has yielded double-digit increases in homicide rates over recent quarters (after five years when murders were reduced by more than two-thirds).

Keep Up the Fight Against Crime

Could we again begin to see "No Radio" signs in American neighborhoods? Given our big new investments in prisons, police, and the like, it will take real effort to throw away the law and order progress won over the last two decades. But if we lose our hard-won sense of realism, and let the fight against crime be undercut by ideologues, we could slip back to the bad old days much faster than many people realize. The choice is ours.

"It's folly to overly rely on an adversarial, alienating, demoralizing criminal justice system."

Crime Policies Should Emphasize Prevention over Punishment

Gene Stephens

Gene Stephens is an associate editor of *USA Today* and a professor of criminal justice at the University of South Carolina, Columbia. He argues in the following viewpoint that the decline in crime since the 1990s is due to the movement toward proactive, community-oriented policing (COP), in which police work with communities to develop programs to cure community ills—such as alcoholism, drug abuse, and unemployment—to prevent crime before it happens. When crime does occur, Stephens writes, the emphasis should be on restoring the health of the community rather than punishing individuals. Stephens believes that this approach is much more effective than that of previous decades, in which police departments often had an adversarial relationship with citizens and crime-control efforts emphasized punishing criminals after the fact.

As you read, consider the following questions:

1. What formula does Stephens say has long been used by crime-prevention researchers?
2. According to the National Institute of Justice report cited by the author, what are some of the crime-control programs of the past that have failed?
3. What are the first and second priorities of restorative justice, as described by Stephens?

P roactive is not merely a buzzword in the American criminal justice system today. It appears to be the key to a successful future in crime prevention and control.

Where police aggressively conduct needs analyses and work with citizens and social service groups to contain crime-breeding situations, street crime rates drop, often dramatically. Similarly, where alternative dispute resolution methods such as mediation, arbitration, and offender-victim conferencing are substituted for adversarial court proceedings to handle the majority of cases—crimes involving people who know one another—victims and community are compensated by offenders who are simultaneously reclaimed through community-developed programs, curtailing future crime.

The Failed "Get Tough" Approach

The major stumbling blocks that could slow this trend are hanging on to old attitudes about crime and punishment and their companion war-model methods of "fighting" crime that have resulted in development of massive criminal justice industrial complexes in nations such as the U.S. Police, courts, and corrections are big business and are not likely to go away or voluntarily accept a diminished role. As long as the emphasis is on repressing crime by catching and punishing individual offenders, a little success (such as currently falling "street" crime rates) will result in the criminal justice complex lobbying for more crimes to feed its monetary needs to support its huge overhead—millions of employees, structures ranging from courthouses to jails and prisons, and equipment from police cruisers to body armor and a plethora of weaponry. Some see the current drug war as an example of a social/medical problem being criminalized to provide billions in funding for criminal justice.

In fact, research indicates the current falling street crime rate is not a result of the reactive war model methods at all. Whereas "get tough" advocates cite the "three strikes" laws and the bulging prison population as reasons for the dramatic decreases, the statistics tell a different story.

For decades, the cleared-by-arrest rate reported in the Federal Bureau of Investigation's Uniform Crime Reports for the eight major crimes has continuously been in the 20%

range, meaning just one in five major crimes lead to an arrest of a suspect—hardly enough to strike fear into the hearts of would-be offenders, and certainly not enough to deter them or prevent crime.

As for the offenders behind bars, 25% in state prisons are there on drug convictions, as are a whopping 80% in Federal prisons. The overwhelming majority of these inmates are addicts serving time for possession of illegal drugs, as dealers are much more difficult to capture and convict. The increase in drug offenders accounts for most of the prison population explosion.

Citizens and Police Working Together

The real change in the 1990s and continuing today has been the citizen response to crime, spearheaded by community action. A majority of the nation's police agencies aspire to be model community-oriented police (COP) operations, and well over 1,000 alternative dispute resolution programs handle criminal as well as civil complaints. While most efforts are far from the headlines and newscasts, they appear to be quietly transforming America into an effective, efficient crime preventing and controlling society. It is these crimes prevented that are reflected in statistics as nonevents—thus lowering overall crime rates.

If crime does not occur, tremendous savings result. There is no harm to victims, offenders, or community, and no private or public dollars are necessary to repair harm and extract "justice." Beyond this, no socioeconomic costs are created by trauma, fear, and distress. Possibly even more important, the criminal justice industrial complex is funded for doing something positive for the citizenry, rather than left embroiled in what many see as race/class warfare in the streets.

The formula of desire + opportunity = crime has long been used in the crime prevention field, but the emphasis has traditionally been on opportunity reduction through target hardening via approaches such as installing better locks and alarms and avoiding being out alone after dark. While such tactics have been successful in reducing crime, they have extracted a heavy cost on individuals and society, as concerned citizens have been encouraged to fear and distrust one another.

The desire portion of the equation has just begun to gain attention, as the assumption has been that swift, severe, and harsh punishment of the offender would deter crime and thus reduce desire. However, research indicates punishment neither deters nor lessens crime by those caught and convicted. In fact, it often leads to increased criminal activity by the angry recipients. Yet, the equation still appears to be workable as the approach is modified by placing emphasis on proactive prevention to reduce criminal desire, rather than the reactive method of hiding behind locked doors and harshly punishing the relatively few caught offenders. . . .

What Works, What Doesn't, and What's Promising

So what does work and what is promising in the future for the prevention and control of crime, while still meeting the requirements of justice and civil liberties? Since the mid 1990s, the National Institute of Justice [NIJ] of the U.S. Department of Justice has sponsored and evaluated numerous crime prevention initiatives. In a landmark study—a result of Federal legislation requiring a scientific review of these programs—NIJ published *Preventing Crime: What Works, What Doesn't, What's Promising.* The "what works" list is relatively short, but significantly includes desire reduction programs such as having nurses and other health/social work professionals frequently visit and assist infants in troubled homes; provide classes and weekly home visits by teachers for preschoolers in these troubled homes; implement family therapy and parent training for delinquents and at-risk (of becoming delinquent) adolescents; coach at-risk youth in "thinking skills"; and develop drug treatment and vocational training for convicted offenders. Opportunity reduction programs indicating success involved extra police patrols in high-crime "hot spots" and monitoring by specialized police units of high-risk repeat offenders.

The "what's promising" list was much longer and included a combination of proactive approaches such as "polite" field interrogations of suspicious persons; police showing greater respect to arrested suspects (found to demonstrate promise of reducing repeat offending); gang monitoring by community workers and probation officers as well as police; and community-based mentoring by Big Brothers/Big Sisters of America. Other promising initiatives included community-based after-school recreation programs; "schools within schools" that group students into smaller units for more individual attention; Job Corps residential training programs for at-risk youth; enterprise zones to reduce unemployment; redesigned layout of retail stores to thwart shoplifting; improved management of bar and tavern staffs to curb violence and driving under the influence of alcohol; metal detectors in public buildings; street closures, barricades, and rerouting to reduce violence and burglary in communities; problem-solving analysis unique to the crime situation at each location (a requirement of any effective COP endeavor); proactive arrests for carrying concealed weapons; special drug courts to give more attention to individual offenders; intensive supervision and aftercare of juvenile offenders; and fines for criminal acts (in addition to incarceration in serious cases).

The largest list, though, was of programs that did not seem to work. For example, it was discovered that community mobilization (such as a Neighborhood Crime Watch) which worked well in middle-income communities did not succeed in high-crime poverty areas because neighbors often did not know and/or trust one another, and, indeed, were the persons most likely to commit crimes against each other. Arrests of juveniles for minor offenses and arrests of unemployed domestic assault suspects were found ineffective, as juveniles often committed new offenses after contact with the system and unemployed abusers went back to the household angry and still jobless. Deterrence efforts such as correctional boot camps and "Scared Straight" programs (where minor juvenile and youthful offenders visit adult prisons) were also found to be ineffective. Short-term job training, rehabilitation, and treatment programs—for juveniles and adults—proved to be inadequate, while longer-term, more-intensive efforts showed "promise.". . .

The academic researchers were careful to avoid any sweeping conclusions from this first review of more than 500 crime prevention programs, but it appeared that early intervention and proactive prevention show the most promise, along with intensive training and treatment for those already at risk or in trouble. Beyond this, community-initiated programs fare better than government-created efforts, and partnerships to provide needed services through existing, established programs are more effective and efficient than starting new governmental programs. . . .

Community-Oriented Policing

The community-oriented policing movement is actually a return to roots, as the father of public policing, Sir Robert Peel, established the basic philosophy and principles for the new profession in setting up the first agency in London in 1829. The duty of police is to prevent crime, Peel declared, adding that the best indicator of success is the absence of crime. Thus, he called his police peace officers.

Community policing requires partnerships that include all public and private agencies in the jurisdiction as well as active participation by community residents. Under ideal conditions, citizens lead the effort to analyze neighborhood needs and set priorities for dealing with crime-breeding situations. COP is a philosophy, rather than specific tactics, as each community must determine its agenda to create its own plan and programs.

In successful COP efforts, crime control (war model) methods—imposed authority, intimidation, demand for compliance, reaction to crime—are replaced by prevention (peace model) methods such as collaborating with the community, establishing trust, sharing power, and implementing proactive crime-prevention centered on seeking out and alleviating problems that cause or lead to crime.

Restorative Justice

Even the best proactive efforts of a community and the police will not be enough to prevent crime in all situations. When crime does occur, restorative justice offers a proactive alternative. Here again, the new approach is in fact a "return to the future" idea, since nonadversarial, consensus-based tribunals and penalties were used in tribes and small communities around the world before "civilization" brought structured legal systems. Emphasis under tribal justice was usually on protection of the community, problem solving, and equity, rather than imposed penalties after adversarial proceedings. A Native American judge commented in Washington, D.C., after a three-day restorative justice conference sponsored by NIJ: "You people [European settlers] came to this country and made us establish your courts and your justice system, and now you're telling us to go back to what we did before you arrived." While favoring the "return to justice," he was perplexed by the historical context.

A LOW CRIME RATE — AT A HIGH PRICE

Three Strikes

Increased Police presence

expanded Sentencing for drug offenses

Zero tolerance

Mandatory Minimums

Sharpnack. © 1999 by *The Gazette*, Iowa City. Reproduced by permission of the artist.

The philosophical principles underlying restorative justice hold that crime is an offense against human relationships—and against individuals and the community—not governments. Thus, first priority is to assist victims, and second priority is to restore community to the degree possible. To do this, the offender must accept his or her responsibilities to the victim and the community, while the community has responsibility to reclaim and reconcile with the offender as the debt is paid. Finally, partnerships among all stakeholders (victim, offender, community) must be established and maintained.

When fully developed, the restorative justice process begins with a determination of the details of the incident and, if there is harm done and it is attributable to certain person(s), to hold the violator(s) accountable to making restitution to the victim(s) and community. The offender then must be assisted in developing the competency, ability, and desire to live lawfully in the community. Finally, all parties are to be reconciled.

One key assist has come from the American Bar Association, which has provided research and support for alternative dispute resolution programs in the wake of an address to its members in 1984 by Supreme Court Justice Warren Burger, who told the attorneys: "[Courts] ought to be healers of conflict . . . for some disputes, trials will be the only means, but for many claims, trial by adversarial contest must go the way of the ancient trial by blood and battle. Our system is too costly, too painful, too destructive for a truly civilized people. . . ."

The Promise of Success

There are, of course, several obstacles that must be overcome to achieve acceptance of the full scope of the COP-restorative crime prevention model. Primary among them is the requirement of change throughout the current multi-billion-dollar criminal justice complex. Many involved have been comfortable and secure in a system where fear has been used successfully to keep taxpayers' money flowing, force and domination have been used to accomplish crimefighting goals, and individual power has been afforded to employees as well as officials.

Being asked to alleviate fear, identify and assist potential offenders, cure community ills, and share power with many other groups has led to high levels of resistance and even sabotage. For example, after a disastrous shoot-out between law enforcement agents and bank robbers in Hollywood, California, in 1997, many police departments across the country cited the higher firepower of the robbers as undeniable evidence that police must have better weaponry to fight the war on crime. A Federal law allowing police to acquire free-of-charge military surplus provided their departments with automatic weapons, tanks, aircraft, and other high-tech gadgetry. Special Weapons and Tactics squads were revitalized and expanded. (Even some university police established SWAT units.)

Critics say the Hollywood incident should have resulted in a redoubling effort to ferret out the problems that led to the event and address them, as no one wins when "good guys" and "bad guys" accelerate their firepower to shoot it out in the community. After all, most recent analyses of the street crime problem point to gun violence as the only area where the U.S. is completely "off the charts"—leading all other nations in deadly incidents. Other crime is in proportion to the rest of the world.

It seems, however, that the proactive movement is strong enough to withstand resistance and even sabotage. Even those most opposed are often converted after seeing the successes—less crime, reduced fear, revitalized social fabric—in communities adopting this approach.

Consider these two stories. The first comes from a Texas police officer concerning community-oriented policing: "You know, years ago I came off a farm in south Texas and took a job as a city police officer. In my mind, I knew who the bad guys were, and I found a lot of fellow officers who felt the same way. We were out to rid society of these parasites. I policed this way for 15 years, and then a new chief came in and started this new-fangled community policing. He put me in a store-front precinct in a downtown district and had me walking a beat. I was so mad, I just sulked the first year. Well, that got old, so I began to talk to people on my beat. After a while, I learned they were much like me—concerned about their children, worried about drugs, upset about daily problems—and pretty soon I found myself referring these people to agencies that could help and then I began to help myself. Now, for the first time in my career, I feel like something other than a human garbage collector. Before, I rode around in my car all day and jumped out to listen to or grab what I considered human garbage. Now, I see people as just that—people. And the fact I can help them makes me feel good about myself and my job."

The second story comes from Caroline Nicholl of the Washington, D.C., Metropolitan Police Department. Recalling the days when she was chief of police in Milton Keynes in metropolitan London, she told how "shop theft" (the English law that prohibits any theft—burglary, robbery, shoplifting—from a merchant) was a constant problem. "It was the same thing over and over again. We'd arrest a teenager and send him away for awhile and then he'd be back doing the same thing. It was a never-ending cycle and had been going on for years, from one generation to another." Nicholl said that she sensed it was time for an "intervention." So, working on instinct and creativity, she decided to develop a police-offender-victim-community conferencing program. "We told these young offenders we'd drop the current charges if they'd meet with us and just be honest."

Several teens accepted the deal and, after numerous sessions with victims, offenders, neighbors, community leaders, and police, the dimensions of the shop theft problem was revealed. Major factors included alcoholism within families, unemployment, lack of after-school activities, and just plain boredom. "We set to work on those problems with full cooperation of community leaders and brought in treatment, job opportunities, and after-school programs. We used the same funds we'd been using to enforce the shop theft laws and detain the offenders, plus we had community contributions of time and effort. Today, [that area of London] simply [doesn't] have a shop theft problem. If the problem is getting bigger, why continue the same approach? It's folly to overly rely on an adversarial, alienating, demoralizing criminal justice system."

Periodical Bibliography

The following articles have been selected to supplement the diverse views presented in this chapter.

John Cloud	"Guarding Death's Door," *Time*, July 14, 2003.
Economist	"The Cruel and Ever More Unusual Punishment," May 15, 1999.
Steven W. Hawkins	"It Is Immoral and Ineffective," *World & I*, September 2002.
Jen Joynt and Carrie Shuchart	"Mortal Justice: The Demography of the Death Penalty," *Atlantic Monthly*, March 2003.
Eli Lehrer	"Communities and Cops Join Forces," *Insight on the News*, January 25, 1999.
Michael Massing	"New Ideas for Ending the War on Drugs," *Nation*, September 20, 1999.
National Review	"The Capital Question," July 17, 2000.
George E. Pataki	"Death Penalty Is a Deterrent," *USA Today*, March 1997.
Paul H. Robinson	"Crime, Punishment, and Prevention," *Public Interest*, Winter 2001.
David C. Slade	"Run, It's the Cops!: Police: Protector or Enemy in High Crime Neighborhoods?" *World & I*, December 1999.
Suzanne Smalley and Debra Rosenberg	"'I Felt Like I Wanted to Hurt People': Emergency Rooms Report the Violent Return of PCP," *Newsweek*, July 22, 2002.
Gene Stephens	"Global Trends in Crime," *Futurist*, May/June 2003.
Margaret Talbot	"Catch and Release," *Atlantic Monthly*, January/February 2003.
Katherine Van Wormer	"Restoring Justice," *USA Today*, November 2001.

For Further Discussion

Chapter 1

1. To support his argument that poverty contributes to crime, George Winslow offers information on national crime rates and economic trends throughout the twentieth century. In contrast, Eli Lehrer, in arguing that reducing crime can alleviate poverty, provides information on nine small neighborhoods and how economic trends have affected crime rates in the 1990s. Whose use of evidence do you find most persuasive, and why?

2. Daphne Lavers contends that media violence may incite real-life violent crime while Maggie Cutler argues that real-life experiences are much more important in determining whether an individual becomes prone to violence. Which viewpoint comes closest to your own views? Could both viewpoints be right? Explain your answer.

3. Dan P. Alsobrooks believes that the criminal justice system should target drug dealers and abusers because of the harm that drug abuse does to individuals and society. The Sentencing Project, on the other hand, argues that the war on drugs has itself harmed society. What types of evidence does each author use to support the claims being made? Which do you find more convincing?

Chapter 2

1. Garen Wintemute and James B. Jacobs discuss some of the same policies in their viewpoints. List these initiatives and discuss how the two authors differ in their views of the policies.

2. Steven Riczo cites a variety of statistics to show that gun ownership is dangerous and ineffective in protecting individuals against crime. What evidence does John R. Lott Jr. offer to refute these claims? Whose arguments are more convincing, and why?

Chapter 3

1. Based on the arguments presented by the *Economist* and Jeff Jacoby, do you feel that America's incarceration rates are too high? Why or why not?

2. What is meant by the term "racial profiling"? Do you feel that James B. Forman Jr. and Heather MacDonald interpret the term differently in their viewpoints? Explain your answer.

3. Patrick T. McCormick contends that adolescents think and judge differently than do adults. Explain whether you agree or disagree with this claim. Also discuss if such a difference, as-

suming it exists, should affect how the criminal justice system treats adolescents.

Chapter 4

1. Do you feel that the death penalty is justified? How did the viewpoints by William Tucker and Nat Hentoff influence your opinion?

2. Karl Zinsmeister favors a more conservative "get tough" approach to crime while Gene Stephens endorses more liberal, innovative policies. Which viewpoint comes closer to your own view of how society should deal with crime? Explain your answer, using specific examples from the viewpoints.

Organizations to Contact

The editors have compiled the following list of organizations concerned with the issues debated in this book. The descriptions are derived from materials provided by the organizations. All have publications or information available for interested readers. The list was compiled on the date of publication of the present volume; the information provided here may change. Be aware that many organizations take several weeks or longer to respond to inquiries, so allow as much time as possible.

American Civil Liberties Union (ACLU)
132 W. 43rd St., New York, NY 10036
(212) 944-9800 • fax: (212) 869-9065
Web site: www.aclu.org
The ACLU champions the rights set forth in the U.S. Constitution. The ACLU opposes racial profiling, the death penalty, and the treatment of juvenile offenders as adults. The organization also believes that mandatory minimum sentencing laws, "three-strikes" laws, and harsh penalties for nonviolent drug offenses are unjust. ACLU publishes the semiannual *Civil Liberties* in addition to policy statements and reports.

American Enterprise Institute (AEI)
1150 17th St. NW, Washington, DC 20036
(202) 862-5800 • (202) 862-7177
Web site: www.aei.org
The American Enterprise Institute for Public Policy Research is a scholarly research institute that is dedicated to preserving limited government and private enterprise. The institute opposes gun control, believes in individual responsibility, and promotes strict policing and punishment policies. It publishes *American Enterprise*, a monthly magazine, and many opinion pieces on crime and law enforcement are available on the AEI Web site.

Americans for Gun Safety (AGS) and the AGS Foundation
(202) 775-0300
Web sites: www.americansforgunsafety.com
www.agsfoundation.com
Founded in 2000, AGS is a nonpartisan, not-for-profit advocacy organization that supports the rights of law-abiding gun owners and promotes proposals for fighting gun crime and keeping guns out of the hands of criminals and children. The organization's top priorities are closing America's gun show loophole, improving the

background check system for gun purchases, encouraging better enforcement of current gun laws, and promoting gun safety. The AGS Foundation provides background, research, and reference materials to the public and to policy makers on issues relating to gun safety, such as the reports *Broken Records: How America's Faulty Background Check System Allows Criminals to Get Guns* and *Stolen Guns: Arming the Enemy.*

Brady Campaign to Prevent Gun Violence and Brady Center to Prevent Gun Violence

1225 Eye St. NW, Suite 1100, Washington, DC 20005
(202) 898-0792 • (202) 289-7319
Web sites: www.bradycampaign.org • www.bradycenter.com

The Brady Campaign to Prevent Gun Violence was formerly known as Handgun Control, Inc. The campaign works to enact and enforce sensible gun laws, regulations, and public policies through grassroots activism, electing pro–gun control public officials, and increasing public awareness of gun violence. The Brady Center works to reform the gun industry and educate the public about gun violence through litigation and grassroots mobilization, and works to enact and enforce regulations to reduce gun violence including regulations governing the gun industry. The Brady Campaign Web site offers dozens of issue briefs, fact sheets, legislative updates, and links to news stories on gun control.

Cato Institute

1000 Massachusetts Ave. NW, Washington, DC 20001
(202) 842-0200 • fax: (202) 842-3490
Web site: www.cato.org

The Cato Institute is a libertarian public policy research foundation. It evaluates government policies and offers reform proposals and commentary on its Web site. The institute opposes gun control and the federal war on drugs, and supports reform of the U.S. prison system. Its publications include the Cato Policy Analysis series of reports, which are available online and include *Fighting Back: Crime, Self-Defense, and the Right to Carry a Handgun*, *Trust the People: The Case Against Gun Control*, and *Warrior Cops: The Ominous Growth of Paramilitarism in American Police Departments*. It also publishes the magazine *Regulation*, the *Cato Policy Report*, and many books.

Coalition to Stop Gun Violence (CSGV)

1000 16th St. NW, Suite 603, Washington, DC 20002
(202) 530-0340 • fax: (202) 530-0331
Web site: www.csgv.org

The CSGV lobbies at the local, state, and federal levels to ban the sale of handguns to individuals and to institute licensing and registration of all firearms. It also litigates cases against firearms makers. Its publications include various informational sheets on gun violence and the *Annual Citizens' Conference to Stop Gun Violence Briefing Book*, a compendium of gun control fact sheets, arguments, and resources.

Death Penalty Information Center (DPIC)
1320 18th St. NW, 5th Floor, Washington, DC 20036
(202) 293-6970
Web site: www.deathpenaltyinfo.org

The DPIC is a nonprofit organization that opposes capital punishment. Through its Web site, DPIC provides analysis and information on issues concerning the death penalty, such as the reports *International Perspectives on the Death Penalty: A Costly Isolation for the U.S.* and *The Death Penalty in Black & White: Who Lives, Who Dies, Who Decides.*

National Center on Institutions and Alternatives (NCIA)
3125 Mt. Vernon Ave., Alexandria, VA 22305
(703) 684-0373
Web site: www.ncianet.org

NCIA works to reduce the number of people institutionalized in prisons and mental hospitals. It favors the least restrictive forms of detention for juvenile offenders, opposes sentencing juveniles as adults, and advocates for serious reform of the U.S. prison system. The NCIA Web site offers numerous reports and articles, including *Masking the Divide: How Officially Reported Prison Statistics Distort the Racial and Ethnic Realities of Prison Growth* and "Youth Homicide: Keeping Perspective on How Many Children Kill."

National Institute of Justice (NIJ)
National Criminal Justice Reference Service (NCJRS)
Box 6000, Rockville, MD 20849
(301) 519-5500 • (800) 851-3420
Web site: www.ncjrs.org

A component of the Office of Justice Programs of the U.S. Department of Justice, the NIJ supports research on crime, criminal behavior, and crime prevention. The National Criminal Justice Reference Service acts as a clearinghouse that provides information and research about criminal justice. Its publications include the report *Fighting Urban Crime: The Evolution of Federal-Local Col-*

laboration, the yearly *Compendium of Federal Justice Statistics*, and the report *Capital Punishment 2002*.

National Rifle Association of America (NRA)
11250 Waples Mill Rd., Fairfax, VA 22030
(703) 267-1000
Web site: www.nra.org

The NRA is America's largest organization of gun owners. It is also the primary lobbying group for those who oppose gun control laws. The NRA believes that such laws violate the U.S. Constitution and do nothing to reduce crime. In addition to its monthly magazines *America's 1st Freedom, American Rifleman, American Hunter, InSights*, and *Shooting Sports USA*, the NRA publishes numerous books, bibliographies, reports, and pamphlets on gun ownership, gun safety, and gun control.

Sentencing Project
514 Tenth St. NW, Suite 1000, Washington, DC 20004
(202) 628-0871
Web site: www.sentencingproject.org

The Sentencing Project is a nonprofit organization that promotes reduced reliance on incarceration and increased use of more humane alternatives to deal with crime. The project's Web site offers numerous briefing sheets and reports on issues such as sentencing law and policy, racial disparities in the criminal justice system, treating juvenile offenders as adults, and the impact of U.S. drug policy on the prison system.

Violence Policy Center
2000 P St. NW, Suite 200, Washington, DC 20036
(202) 822-8200 • fax: (202) 822-8202
Web site: www.vpc.org

The Violence Policy Center is an educational foundation that conducts research on firearms violence. It works to educate the public concerning the dangers of guns and supports gun control measures. The center's publications include the reports *When Men Murder Women: An Analysis of 2001 Homicide Data, Handgun Licensing and Registration: What It Can and Cannot Do*, and *License to Kill IV: More Guns, More Crime*.

Bibliography of Books

Katherine Beckett
and Theodore Sasson

The Politics of Injustice: Crime and Punishment in America. Thousand Oaks, CA: Pine Forge Press, 2000.

Alfred Blumstein and
Joel Wallman, eds.

The Crime Drop in America. New York: Cambridge University Press, 2000.

John M. Bruce and
Clyde Wilcox

The Changing Politics of Gun Control. Lanham, MD: Rowman & Littlefield, 1998.

David Cole

No Equal Justice: Race and Class in the American Criminal Justice System. New York: New Press, 1999.

Philip J. Cook and
Jens Ludwig

Gun Violence: The Real Costs. New York: Oxford University Press, 2000.

Chris Crowther

Policing Urban Poverty. New York: St. Martin's Press, 2000.

Alexander DeConde

Gun Violence in America: The Struggle for Control. Boston: Northeastern University Press, 2001.

Jan E. Dizard,
Robert Merril Muth,
and Stephen P.
Andrews Jr., eds.

Guns in America: A Reader. New York: New York University Press, 1999.

Barry C. Feld

Bad Kids: Race and the Transformation of the Juvenile Court. New York: Oxford University Press, 1999.

Darin D. Frederickson
and Raymond P.
Siljander

Racial Profiling. Springfield, IL: Charles C. Thomas, 2002.

John R. Fuller and
Eric W. Hickey, eds.

Controversial Issues in Criminology. Boston: Allyn and Bacon, 1999.

David Garland

The Culture of Control: Crime and Social Order in Contemporary Society. Chicago: University of Chicago Press, 2001.

Thomas Grisso and
Robert G. Schwartz,
eds.

Youth on Trial: A Developmental Perspective on Juvenile Justice. Chicago: University of Chicago Press, 2000.

Bernard E. Harcourt

Illusion of Order: The False Promise of Broken Windows Policing. Cambridge, MA: Harvard University Press, 2001.

David A. Harris

Profiles in Injustice: Why Racial Profiling Cannot Work. New York: New Press, 2002.

Tara Herivel and Paul Wright, eds.	*Prison Nation: The Warehousing of America's Poor.* New York: Routledge, 2003.
James B. Jacobs	*Can Gun Control Work?* New York: Oxford University Press, 2002.
George L. Kelling	*Fixing Broken Windows: Restoring Order and Reducing Crime in Our Communities.* New York: Free Press, 1996.
Gary Kleck and Don B. Kates Jr.	*Armed: New Perspectives on Gun Control.* Amherst, NY: Prometheus Books, 2001.
Ann Chih Lin, ed.	*Capital Punishment.* Washington, DC: CQ Press, 2002.
John R. Lott Jr.	*More Guns, Less Crime: Understanding Crime and Gun-Control Laws.* New York: New York University Press, 2002.
Jens Ludwig and Philip J. Cook, eds.	*Evaluating Gun Policy: Effects on Crime and Violence.* Washington, DC: Brookings Institution Press, 2003.
Michael W. Markowitz and Delores D. Jones-Brown, eds.	*The System in Black and White: Exploring the Connections Between Race, Crime, and Justice.* Westport, CT: Praeger, 2000.
Deborah Mitchell Robinson and M.L. Dantzker, eds.	*Policing and Crime Prevention.* Upper Saddle River, NJ: Prentice-Hall, 2002.
Henry Ruth and Kevin R. Reitz	*The Challenge of Crime: Rethinking Our Response.* Cambridge, MA: Harvard University Press, 2003.
Peter Squires	*Gun Culture or Gun Control: Firearms, Violence, and Society.* New York: Routledge, 2000.
Josh Sugarmann	*Every Handgun Is Aimed at You: The Case for Banning Handguns.* New York: New Press, 2001.
Ralph B. Taylor	*Breaking Away from Broken Windows: Baltimore Neighborhoods and the Nationwide Fight Against Crime, Grime, Fear, and Decline.* Boulder, CO: Westview Press, 2001.
Samuel Walker, Cassia Spohn, and Miriam DeLone	*The Color of Justice: Race, Ethnicity, and Crime in America.* Belmont, CA: Wadsworth Thomson Learning, 2000.
Franklin E. Zimring and Gordon Hawkins	*Crime Is Not the Problem: Lethal Violence in America.* New York: Oxford University Press, 1997.

Index